Praise for *Thriving in Chaos*

This was a quick read! I'm so impressed and relieved that this is going into existence. The world needs this book.

Jenny Eldredge, nonprofit executive

I love the book. It's so good. I love how it balances practical advice with clear, sound information. I absolutely love the PACE acronym. I think it's a great tool and so applicable to this phase of life. I'm already thinking of ways I could use the book with my clients' children! 🖤 🖤 🖤

Susan Larson, Owner, SYNERGY HomeCare of Southern Twin Cities

I really enjoyed the book which provided such valuable information about aging. Dealing with aging parents is new for many going through the process for the first time and knowing we are not alone is comforting. Starting a movement talking about these matters that affect so many is greatly needed. Thank you, Heather and Jayne, for this very insightful information. I will be recommending this book to the adult children of my senior clients.

Carey Lindeman, Founder of Promise Care, a Private Home Care and Family Care Consultant.

Heather and Jayne share their journeys with honesty, compassion, and hope in this heartfelt book. Blending real-life stories, facts, and reflections, they provide tools, encouragement, and "glimmers of strength" to help navigate the challenges of caring for aging parents—an invaluable resource for anyone on this path.

Heather Tran, Executive Director, A Better Society

NAVIGATING THE CHALLENGES OF
AGING PARENTS

THRIVING
IN
CHAOS

HEATHER DURENBERGER, MA, MBA
AND JAYNE DOW LARKIN

Legal & Disclaimer

This guide's content and information are consistent and truthful, and they have been provided for informational, educational, and business purposes only.

As we dive into the guide—we're not legal, financial, or mental health professionals, and we're not here to give you any formal advice. This guide is about sharing our experiences and the things that have helped us navigate our tough times. We hope you find something that resonates with you here, but always remember to contact a professional for any serious concerns or decisions. We're just here to share our journey and offer some support along the way.

Dedication

In our world, we don't talk about the struggles of caring for our aging parents. Often, this journey arrives with a huge splash and unfolds with deep solitude as you struggle through the tumultuous storms of adversity. In my experience, it is grueling, isolating, and incredibly challenging.

This guide is dedicated to everyone supporting aging parents, especially those struggling and suffering in silence. We want to give you glimmers of strength that will light your way through the sometimes dark and weary places. We hope you find the tools to navigate this path and learn to support one another better. We seek to lift our voices to make the world better for our children so that one day when they begin caregiving for our generation, they will do so in a healthier way.

Wherever you are on this path, welcome; we are glad you are here. May this guide illuminate your way, empower your heart, and lead you to peace and wholeness in the challenges of caring for your aging parents.

Acknowledgment

We want to express our heartfelt thanks to our family and friends who have stood by us throughout this journey of caring for our aging parents. This experience has strengthened us in ways we never imagined, and your love and support have made what seemed impossible possible.

We want to take a moment to extend our deepest gratitude to those who dedicate their lives to working with older adults every day. Your compassion, patience, and unwavering commitment to caring for others is inspiring.

To family members who support their loved ones with the help of professional caregivers, your strength and love shine brightly in a challenging space. We are humbled by the opportunity to serve and share our experiences with you. It's an honor to be part of a community that values kindness, respect, and the dignity of every individual. Thank you for all that you do.

AUTHOR'S NOTE

We recognize that the journey of caring for an aging parent or loved one is deeply personal and shaped by our individual identities. We are committed to honoring diverse stories and ensuring that this space remains inclusive, respectful, and supportive for all.

Contents

Introduction

The Journey from Surviving to Thriving

I have had a front-row seat to caregiving for as long as I can remember being on this earth. As a pastor's daughter, I jumped at the opportunity to accompany my dad in his visitation with congregation members. We visited nursing homes, seniors who were "shut-in" their homes, people battling chronic and terminal illnesses, as well as innumerable hospital visitations. My heart was drawn to those in need as I accompanied him on these visits, witnessing the beauty and challenges of their lives. Whenever I heard the phone ring, I'd be ready to jump into his green Datsun to visit whoever needed a pastoral visit.

Growing up in this space where these outward expressions of caring for others lay the hidden realities within the four walls of my childhood home. Behind closed doors, my parents grappled with significant mental health challenges, thrusting me into a role of caregiving far more intimate and personal than I could have ever imagined. A picture hangs in my upstairs hallway that I clearly remember being taken. It's me sitting in the front garden of our home with a big smile. I was eight years old. Soon after that picture was taken, the realities of my parents' challenges became much more straightforward. I took on the responsibility as a child to support my parents and younger siblings, which was heavy. At this point in my life and through these experiences, I began to think about what it's like to step into the role of caregiving. Within the confines of these private struggles, the seeds of my caregiving journey were sown, shaping my understanding of empathy, resilience, and the transformative power of compassion.

These experiences sculpted the framework of my understanding, leading me to embrace a path of service and compassion. Through the storms of life, from ministry work to personal trials, I've been forged into one who cares for others with a mission—to illuminate the path for others who come behind me amid the darkness. I hope that sharing my stories and my path through them might provide a glimmer of light and encouragement for those who come behind me or are walking right alongside me.

Reflecting on the journey, I realized that caring for someone is not just about tending to the physical needs of our loved ones. It's about navigating the turbulent waters of the heart and soul, finding peace in the chaos, and finding joy in the storm. It's about building resilience, forging connections, and discovering the depths of our strength.

I've honed my skills each year, drawing from my biopsychology and business administration education and my lived experience.

And through it all, my faith has been my steadfast companion, offering solace in moments of doubt and lighting the path forward. Now, I find myself extending my hand to those on a similar journey, hoping to illuminate and give you language for the path you are walking.

Until you are caring for your aging parents, it is hard to imagine how all-encompassing this new responsibility becomes. Let me tell you, caring for aging parents is a whole new level of challenge. I ask you to explore what it entails. This is an excellent exercise to stop and reflect. Where am I currently? What isn't even on my radar?

For some, the journey begins gradually, with subtle shifts in roles and responsibilities within the family unit. For others, it arrives suddenly, like a bolt of lightning illuminating the path ahead. Whether gradual or abrupt, the call to care compels us to confront the realities of illness, aging, or disability and respond with love, compassion, and courage.

As the gravity of our caregiving responsibilities settles upon our shoulders, we are confronted with the profound realization that we are now caring for our aging parents. This realization marks a significant shift in our identities as we transition from being sons, daughters, spouses, or siblings to becoming those who care for our parents, entrusted with the sacred task of tending to the needs of loved ones with humility, grace, and compassion.

As adult children, most of us think we know what to expect. As those who have walked this path, we humbly assert that our world is naïve in that assumption. Many of our parents think that by having an estate plan or a will in place, they are covered. Many even give themselves bonus points for having a healthcare directive with final wishes. We say to ourselves, "Phew, I am covered. The boxes are checked, and I am ready."

Either you are already in the thick of it and know this does not even scratch the surface of being prepared to care for your aging parent, or you are just learning or getting started in this journey with your aging parent, in which case—we hate to break it to you—this is not even close to being prepared.

Our goal in capturing the collective experiences, stories, and knowledge from so many and sharing it in this guide is to help you better prepare and better understand the reality of what awaits you and your aging parents.

We are grateful that you are joining us on this journey into the heart of caring for aging parents, where we are all in some way challenged, honed, and transformed. We are sending you light and love, healing, and hope along your way.

CHAPTER 1

Changing the Conversation

"Every great dream begins with a dreamer. Always remember, you have within you the strength, the patience, and the passion to reach for the stars to change the world." Harriet Tubman

Over the last two years, we have processed the deep suffering and enduring that comes with life's storms, especially when caring for aging parents.

Together, we have asked profound questions about why we face repeated crises and whether there's a better way to walk this journey. What shifted within us that enabled a different response as these storms continued? How can we share our experiences and help others move beyond merely enduring to truly thriving in the challenges of caring for our aging parents? Through our conversations, we realized the power of our shared learning and new strengths and were driven to share this with others—to empower them to navigate the chaos, stress, and grief with resilience and hope so they, too, can find a better way forward.

The idea that we would be caring for our aging parents and parents-in-law this soon was not even on our radars. It isn't until a storm hits—physical, financial, or emotional—that suddenly, we are caught up in the chaos of a crisis involving our aging parents.

It is a "what the hell" moment for many of us. We are caught entirely off-guard and knocked down by a tidal wave and sometimes a tsunami, where one day, we are thrown into the mix of learning how to navigate the complex space of caring for our aging parents. We have felt the overwhelming pressure of balancing our everyday lives with the increasing demands of caring for our parents in a culture that still acts like this isn't a real-life stage.

We are deeply committed to changing the cultural conversation in our country. This is about starting a movement, doing better for those not yet in the squeeze, and doing better for the next generation. We can do better. We can.

So much of what happens as our parents begin to age is not considered or discussed. We often approach every life stage with careful consideration. How do you enter adult life without first understanding what is required to have a home and job? Or have a child without preparing for it or considering all its needs?

With so many of the needs and tensions of aging parents, we unthinkingly walk into a minefield where we innocently set off mines left and right of all these triggers under the surface that explode, and we never even realize that we are in a minefield in the first place. Like, wait a hot second, how did I get here? And how the hell do I get out of here? Well, you are in the right place.

We are here to help you NAME IT, FRAME IT, and EMBRACE IT. We give you the language to process and understand what you need to know regarding the realities of aging parents.

We share the foundations of this transitory phase, mapping the tensions you are feeling with your aging parents and giving you a model for embracing each storm with the knowledge that you and your loved one will be okay. Your understanding of the phase of life you are entering is key. You can survive this!

CHAPTER 2

A New Stage of Senior Adulthood

"After driving with my dad, I asked him if he had given any thought to finding some support with driving as he was having difficulty recalling directions and how to get familiar places. He blew a gasket; I won't make that mistake again." Mom of three, age 53.

"I've noticed my mom is repeating herself and asking me the same questions repeatedly. Sometimes even on the same phone call. I've tried to raise my concerns with her, but she says it is none of my business. She is more on edge and shorter with me than I have ever seen her. I am at a loss, and I am worried about her." Mom of one, age 53.

Aging can be a long and complicated process, and an aging person's needs can change anytime. In some cases, seniors are relatively stable in their physical and cognitive health for years. Other times, though, they may experience a rapid decline in health. The complexity we are learning to navigate as adult children is the many unknowns accompanying the aging process. In addition to the unknowns is the fact that our world doesn't talk about aging, and it's almost like we are ashamed or embarrassed by this very natural period of our lives. This period in life is also more nuanced and complex than just "aging" or "getting old." It has a progression and often a pattern. To really process the experience of aging, it is better if we can identify and name the facets of aging.

Dr. Mark Frankel, clinical psychologist, and pioneer in supporting families with eldercare challenges, identified the five stages of aging: Self-Sufficiency, Interdependence, Dependency, Crisis Management, and End of Life.

Five Stages of Aging

Self Sufficiency	Interdependence	Dependence	Crisis Management	End of Life
People live independently and can complete their activities of daily living with ease.	They can still live alone safely and can complete most of their usual activities without help. However, they do need some degree of care from family or friends.	At this stage, an aging person can no longer live on their own safely.	This stage occurs when an aging person needs immediate and ongoing medical support.	The aging person is nearing their final days choosing to stop receiving medical treatment or enter hospice care.

The Need to be Reliant on Others Increases

As we age, our level of independence typically declines, leading to an increased need for support. This shift can be challenging to accept, both for the aging individual and their family members. The desire to maintain autonomy is vital, especially for those with high independence. However, as physical, and cognitive functions begin to wane, the need for assistance becomes more pronounced. This transition often creates friction between aging parents and their children, who may be stepping into caregiving roles.

There is often a pivotal moment when the level of independence shifts from self-sufficiency into inter-dependence. This transition is not always smooth and can bring a range of emotional tensions and strains. Often, this phase begins with a crisis or storm.

Five Stages of Aging

Self Sufficiency	Interdependence	Dependence	Crisis Management	End of Life

The Need to be Reliant on Others Increases

It may also start with clues that we, as adult children, begin noticing, and our inquiries are often met with defiance and opposition from our aging parents. Our gut tells us something is changing; we can feel it and don't have words for it. When our guts are yelling at us that something is off or that something is going to happen, but again, our current culture lacks the framework or language to help us articulate this concern.

Much like the rebellious and tumultuous phase of adolescence, our aging parents may resist this change, clinging to their independence even as their ability to manage daily tasks diminishes. This period is marked by a gradual role reversal, where the child provides or coordinates more and more support, and the parent increasingly relies on their support.

This time period looks and feels a lot like the transitional stage of physical and psychological development that generally occurs during the period from puberty to adulthood, whereas here, it is again a transitional stage that is occurring in reverse as physical and psychological development is in decline.

We call it the Adolescence of Aging. It is a parallel to the transition from childhood to adulthood, marked by adolescence of youth, and the transition from independence to dependence many people experience as they age. Both stages involve significant changes in physical and cognitive abilities, emotional adjustments, and shifts in social roles.

Five Stages of Aging

Self Sufficiency	Interdependence	Dependence	Crisis Management	End of Life

Adolescence OF Aging +

The Need to be Reliant on Others Increases

This role reversal can be emotionally challenging for both parties.

For aging parents, the loss of independence can feel like a loss of identity and control, leading to feelings of frustration, fear, and even resentment. They may struggle to accept help, insisting they are still capable, even when not. This can lead to conflicts and misunderstandings as children try to balance respecting their parents' autonomy and ensuring their safety and well-being.

For adult children, stepping into caring for an aging parent is often fraught with challenges. The emotional strain of watching a parent decline, coupled with the responsibility of managing their care, can be overwhelming. It's also challenging to navigate the delicate balance between providing support and maintaining the parent's dignity. This tension can strain the relationship, where the parent may feel infantilized or disempowered, and the child may feel burdened or guilt-ridden.

The demands of caring for an aging parent don't exist in a vacuum. For many, these responsibilities come when they are already managing relationships with children at different life stages—toddlers who need constant care, teenagers grappling with their identity crises, or grade school children requiring academic and emotional support. The need to provide care and attention to both aging parents and young children can stretch adult children's emotional resources to the breaking point.

Maintaining healthy relationships with partners, children, and friends while managing these caregiving demands adds another layer of complexity. The challenge becomes even more significant in the absence of spousal support due to a partner's demanding job, emotional distance, or being a single parent. Adult children may find themselves isolated, with little to no time for social connections or self-care, leading to feelings of loneliness and exhaustion.

The emotional labor involved in balancing these relationships can be intense. Adult children may feel torn between the competing needs of their parents, children, and partners, leading to feelings of inadequacy or guilt for not meeting everyone's needs. The stress of maintaining a semblance of normalcy in relationships while dealing with the unpredictability and demands of caregiving can strain even the strongest bonds.

The intersection of these responsibilities—caring for aging parents and raising children—creates a unique and challenging dynamic. The caregiver is often caught in the middle, trying to manage the shifting needs of their parents while still fulfilling their roles as partners, parents, and friends. This balancing act can sometimes feel impossible, leading to a sense of being stretched too thin, with little to no support to alleviate the burden.

Ultimately, the Adolescence of Aging is a phase that requires immense emotional resilience and adaptability. It's a time when the dynamics of relationships are tested, and the roles within the family are redefined. Navigating this period requires practical support and a deep understanding and empathy for the complex emotions involved in this transition.

The Adolescence of Aging is a metaphor that captures the essence of this transition. Just as adolescence is a period of significant change, during which young people navigate the complexities of becoming adults, aging is a time of profound transformation, during which individuals move from a state of independence toward one of increased reliance on others. Emotional turbulence, identity shifts, and the need for adaptation characterize both stages.

By exploring and acknowledging these similarities, we gain insight into the tensions between aging parents and their adult children and develop strategies to navigate these challenges more effectively.

A Moment to Reflect

Let's pause here for a moment and take a deep breath. When you are ready, read on.

What "clues" have you noticed in your own experience that suggest your loved one's needs may be shifting toward greater dependence? Reflect on how these changes have impacted your interactions and the challenges that may have arisen from them.

How do you currently navigate the balance between respecting your parent's independence and ensuring their safety and well-being? Are there strategies from the chapter that might help you manage this delicate balance?

In what ways has your caregiving role impacted your relationship with your parent? Has this role reversal led to any tension, frustration, or miscommunication?

How does the concept of the "Adolescence of Aging" resonate with your experience? Reflect on how understanding this stage as a parallel to adolescence might change how you approach challenges, respect your parent's needs, and maintain compassion.

CHAPTER 3

Surviving the Adolescence of Aging

"*I am not sure who to reach out to or what even to ask. My parents are not themselves; something is off. They say they want to age in place but can't seem to go grocery shopping or even do laundry. I am not even going to think about them doing the laundry. What is going on? Where do we even begin the conversation?*" Son, age 44

"*This past winter break, we went to visit my parents. The last time we were with them was last summer. I don't know what it was, but they struggled with each other and me. They got frustrated quickly, and my mom even told one of my kids to shut up. I almost fainted. I don't know what is happening, but something is not adding up.*" Empty nester, age 53

"*This past Thanksgiving, I watched my mom prepare the annual turkey dinner. This year, she was agitated, seemed confused, and was exhausted. When we offered to help, she got furious and said we didn't understand and should leave the kitchen. I am at a loss.*" Mom of two, Grandmom, age 56

One of the most striking parallels between adolescence and aging is the frustration arising from body and mind changes. Adolescents in youth experience rapid physical growth and hormonal changes that affect their mood, behavior, and self-perception. Similarly, aging individuals face a decline in physical and cognitive abilities, leading to frustration, helplessness, and even anger. These emotional responses are natural reactions to losing control over one's body and mind.

The struggle is often about asserting independence while relying on parents or guardians for guidance and support. This push and pull can lead to conflicts as young people seek to establish their identities and make their own decisions, even as they recognize the need for some level of dependence. In the same way, aging parents may resist their children's increasing support, as it can infringe on their autonomy. This resistance can manifest in various ways, including defiance, irritability, and refusal to accept help.

The tension between aging parents and their children is often rooted in this clash of desires: the aging parent's wish to maintain independence versus the children's concern for their safety and well-being. The emotional and psychological aspects of aging further complicate this dynamic. Aging individuals may experience a loss of independence, physical abilities, cognitive sharpness, and sometimes even social connections. This loss can lead to vulnerability, insecurity, and fear, expressed as resistance to change, or support.

Stepping into caregiving can be equally challenging for adult children, especially when setting boundaries and making decisions for the aging parent. This role reversal can create emotional strain as adult children balance their respect for their parents' autonomy with the need to ensure their safety and well-being. Feelings of guilt, frustration, and sadness can further complicate the situation as they witness their parents' decline.

One key insight is the recognition that many strategies parents use to support their adolescent children can be adapted to help aging parents. Just as parents of teenagers must balance giving their children freedom with providing guidance, adult children of aging parents must balance respecting their parents' autonomy with ensuring they receive the necessary care and support.

Clear and compassionate communication is essential in both scenarios. With adolescents, open dialogue helps build trust and understanding, allowing parents to set boundaries while acknowledging their children's growing need for independence. Similarly, when dealing with aging parents, clear communication can help to alleviate fears, clarify expectations, and reduce misunderstandings. It is important to involve aging parents in decisions about their care as much as possible, ensuring they feel heard and respected.

Setting boundaries is another crucial strategy. For parents of adolescents, setting clear boundaries helps to establish a structure within which the young person can safely explore their independence. For adult children of aging parents, setting boundaries is about balancing providing the necessary support and allowing the parent to maintain control over their life. This might involve negotiating how and when help is provided and ensuring that both parties are comfortable with the arrangements.

Patience and empathy are vital in navigating the Adolescence of Aging. As adolescents test limits and push back against authority, aging parents may resist changes and express frustration. Understanding that these behaviors are often rooted in underlying fears and insecurities can help caregivers approach the situation with compassion rather than confrontation. Recognizing the emotional complexity of aging and addressing it with empathy can ease the transition from independence to increased dependence, reducing tension, and fostering a more positive relationship.

The Adolescence of Aging highlights the importance of providing practical and emotional support. Just like adolescents need guidance in navigating the challenges of growing up and emotional support to help them manage the stress and confusion of this stage of life, aging parents too need practical assistance with daily tasks as well as emotional support to help them cope with the changes they are experiencing. Offering reassurance, validation, and a listening ear can go a long way in helping aging parents feel understood and supported.

It's also important to recognize that just as adolescence in youth is not a uniform experience for all young people, the adolescence in aging varies significantly from person to person. Some individuals may accept the need for increased support with grace, while others may struggle more with losing independence. Understanding the unique needs and personality of the aging parent is critical to providing the right kind of support.

The Adolescence of Aging encourages us to consider the broader societal and cultural factors that influence aging. In many cultures, aging is viewed with reverence and older individuals are respected and valued for their wisdom and experience. In other cultures, aging can be seen as a decline, leading to marginalization and a loss of status. These cultural attitudes can significantly impact how aging individuals perceive themselves and how their families and communities treat them.

Older individuals may feel more valued and supported in cultures where aging is respected, making the transition from independence to dependence easier to navigate. Conversely, in cultures where aging is viewed negatively, the aging individual may struggle more with feelings of worthlessness and fear of becoming a burden. Understanding these cultural dynamics is crucial in providing appropriate support and care for aging parents.

The Adolescence of Aging also prompts us to reflect on the broader implications of this transition for society. As the population ages, the number of individuals experiencing this shift from independence to dependence increases. This demographic shift significantly affects healthcare, social services, and family dynamics. Recognizing and understanding this life stage, policymakers, employers, healthcare providers, and families must develop more effective strategies to support aging individuals and ensure their well-being.

Navigating Tensions in the Adolescence of Aging

As the roles we once knew so well start to change, parents who spend decades telling their kids to eat their vegetables and drive safely suddenly find themselves receiving reminders to take their medication and avoid stairs. The shifting stages of aging—independence to interdependence, dependence, crisis, and finally passing away—stir up tender and unnamed tensions between parents and adult children.

While we have explored these stages, let's dive deeper into what it might feel like for everyone involved, what it might look like, and what the tensions are for the aging parent and the adult children.

Self-Sufficiency

What it looks like: Ah, the golden years of independence! This is when your aging parent insists, they're "just fine" and can handle everything independently. They still drive to the grocery store (even if they accidentally forget a turn signal or two) and swear they can fix that leaky faucet despite needing reading glasses to find the toolbox.

In this stage, aging parents live independently, manage their daily activities, and continue life as they always have. They may be recently retired, enjoying hobbies and community events.

Tensions for the Parent: While parents relish their freedom, they may also begin to feel subtle changes in their health or energy levels. The idea that they might one day need help can lead to denial or resistance to planning for the future.

Tensions for Adult Child: We have felt the overwhelming pressure of balancing our everyday lives with the increasing demands of caring for our parents in a culture that still acts like this isn't a real-life stage. This stage is often reassuring for adult children, but it can also bring quiet anxiety. The child may start to notice signs of aging—forgetfulness, minor falls, or fatigue—that makes them concerned about their parent's long-term independence. However, trying to broach this subject can feel like invading their parent's autonomy.

Easing the Tension: In this stage, it's all about striking the right balance. You might notice subtle changes in your parents, like they're forgetting things or seem more tired, but bringing this up too soon can feel like crossing a line. Instead of rushing into a "fix-it" mode, try approaching things with gentle curiosity. Ask, "How have you been feeling lately?" or "What's been on your mind about the future?" It's a softer way to open the door for these conversations without making them feel like you're questioning their autonomy.

It's also okay to take a step back and observe. Sometimes, we notice things and immediately want to act, but part of supporting our parents at this stage is giving them the space to stay in control. You're planting seeds for future conversations, not pushing them to face everything immediately.

Interdependence

Things get a little more nuanced as time progresses. Interdependence is that murky middle ground where everyone's adjusting to new roles, even if no one wants to admit it. Your parents may now ask for help with small things—like asking you to help open that stubborn jar or fix the iPad that keeps "acting up," for example—but they still maintain a sense of pride and self-sufficiency.

The shift to interdependence is subtle at first. It's easy to think that asking you to install a new smoke alarm is just a one-off favor, but soon, you're fielding daily calls about the internet connection and whether they've seen the remote. The underlying tension here? Parents may feel like their independence is being chipped away while children grapple with the slow reality of this new balancing act.

At this point, parents can still live independently but begin to need assistance with some tasks, like driving, home maintenance, or managing medical appointments. They may rely on adult children or other family members for help.

Tensions for the Parent: The shift to accepting help can be emotionally challenging. Parents may feel frustrated or embarrassed that they can no longer do everything independently. They often resist asking for help, afraid that doing so might signal a loss of control over their lives.

Tensions for the Adult Child: This is where the balancing act intensifies for the adult child. They want to help, but guilt can be associated with being unable to provide all the care their parents need, especially if they live far away or have family and career responsibilities. Conversations about increased support can lead to tension as parents push back against offers of assistance.

Easing the Tension: As your parent needs more help, the tricky part is knowing when to step in or when not to, letting them handle things independently. It can feel awkward—you don't want to hover or make them feel incapable. An excellent way to navigate this is to offer help in small, specific ways. Instead of saying, "Do you need help?" which can feel like you're questioning their abilities, try, "I'm going to the store. Do you want me to grab anything for you?"

Let them maintain as much independence as possible but be present. You're walking alongside them, not taking over the reins. It's about offering support without making them feel like they're losing their grip on their life.

Dependence

Dependence is when the need for help becomes undeniable. Parents may now rely on their adult children for daily tasks, such as driving to appointments, managing medications, or even helping with personal care. This stage often arrives with a sense of loss for parents and a growing responsibility for children.

In this stage, parents often need significant help with daily living activities. This may require home modifications, hiring in-home care, or moving to an assisted living facility. Their independence is fading, but they may still maintain some control over their environment.

Tensions for the Parent: The transition to needing more structured support is a tough pill to swallow. Many parents grieve for the loss of their autonomy and feel that they are becoming a burden. This can manifest as anger, withdrawal, or depression as they wrestle with their identity, shifting from self-sufficiency to needing care.

Tensions for the Adult Child: Adult children often take on a more active caregiving role, and the strain can lead to feeling overwhelmed. If the child suggests moving to assisted living, it can spark defensiveness in the parent, creating emotional conflict. The child may also struggle with guilt, feeling they are abandoning their parent by not providing all the necessary care themselves.

This is where things can get emotional. Your parent is starting to rely on you more heavily, which can stir up many feelings for both of you. For your parent, it's tough to acknowledge they need more help, and for you, stepping into a caregiving role can feel overwhelming.

Easing the Tension: The key here is to recognize that it's okay to feel all the emotions that come with this stage—frustration, sadness, and sometimes even resentment. Permit yourself to feel those things without judgment. But also, don't be afraid to ask for help. You don't have to shoulder everything yourself. Talk to your siblings, reach out to friends, or explore outside caregiving resources. It's not about doing it all alone but finding a rhythm that works for both of you.

Crisis Management

Crises can come in many forms from health emergencies, hospitalizations, or sudden declines that change everything overnight. In this stage, families often enter new emotional territory. Decisions about care may be rushed, tensions flare, and family dynamics that have simmered for decades suddenly boil over.

Here, the tension comes from fear and worry and the rapid transition into decision-making roles that can leave adult children feeling lost. And let's be honest: when siblings are involved, old rivalries resurface. One might insist on the "best" nursing home, while another swears by at-home care—and both claim they know what Mom or Dad "really" wants.

This stage typically follows a significant health event—like a fall, stroke, or the onset of dementia—that requires round-the-clock care. Parents may need skilled nursing or full-time in-home support, and decision-making often shifts to the child or healthcare providers.

Tensions for the Parent: At this point, parents may feel a profound loss of control over their bodies and lives. This sense of helplessness can lead to despair, especially when decisions are made on their behalf. They may feel anger toward their child for making tough decisions, like placing them in a care facility.

Tensions for the Adult Child: Navigating a health crisis can be incredibly stressful for adult children. They are often left to make critical medical and financial decisions for their parent, which can lead to feelings of doubt or guilt. There may be unresolved feelings of grief as they witness their parent's decline, even as they try to manage the day-to-day logistics of care.

When a health crisis hits, everything can feel like it's happening simultaneously. Suddenly, decisions need to be made, and emotions are running high. This is a stage where you'll need to lean into your ability to stay grounded, even when everything feels chaotic.

Easing the Tension: Remember that it's okay not to have all the answers. Allow yourself to ask questions and take things one step at a time. Also, remember that being present for your parent, even in the most minor ways—holding their hand, listening to their fears—can be just as important as the practical decisions you're making. This is a time to embrace vulnerability and lean on your support system. Don't try to be the hero; you're doing enough just by being there.

End of Life

The final stage is often the hardest to prepare for emotionally. While everyone knows it's coming, that doesn't make it easier when it finally arrives. The loss of a parent, especially after years of providing care, can bring a strange mix of relief and grief. And then there's the added layer of family dynamics—reminiscing, unearthing long-buried grievances, and sometimes...finding humor in unexpected places.

As painful as this stage is, it can also be a time of reflection, healing, and connection—albeit with its quirks. One sibling might make a joke at an inappropriate time, trying to break the tension, while another can't stop crying. Meanwhile, parents in their final days may offer sage advice, tender confessions, or... wonder why Mom's glasses are still missing.

In this final stage, parents may be in a nursing home or under full-time care, unable to manage their basic needs. They are entirely dependent on others for their physical well-being.

Tensions for the Parent: For the parent, this is often the most emotionally taxing stage, as they lose almost all personal agency. They may struggle with feelings of worthlessness or experience anxiety about dying. Visits from family members can bring some comfort but may also evoke feelings of sadness or even anger over the loss of their former self.

Tensions for the Adult Child: Seeing a parent in this state can be emotionally devastating. The child may wrestle with feelings of grief and anticipatory loss, along with the emotional and financial burdens of managing long-term care. They may feel guilt over not being able to "fix" things, and tension can arise if the parent expresses dissatisfaction with the care they are receiving.

Easing the Tension: This stage can be challenging but full of opportunities for connection and closure. As your parent nears the end of life, you may feel like there's a race against time—things you want to say, unfinished conversations, or maybe regrets. But here's the truth: there's no right way to go through this. You don't have to have all the perfect words or do everything exactly right. What matters most is that you're present.

Sitting with your parent, sharing memories, or even sitting silently can be significant. It's about creating moments where you're with them without the need to fix or solve anything. This is a stage where the simplest acts of love can have the most significant impact. And remember to take care of yourself, too. Grief can begin long before the actual goodbye, so allow yourself to feel and process as you go.

Shifting through these stages isn't easy. It brings out tension, laughter, tears, and everything in between. But recognizing these transitions for what they are—natural, complicated, and sometimes absurd—can help families find peace.

As we navigate these waters with our aging parents, giving each other space for all the messy emotions that come with it is essential. Because if there's one thing we know about aging and family, life rarely goes according to plan. And maybe that's where the beauty lies—in the shared moments, the awkward conversations, and even with the forgotten TV remote.

Understanding the emotional terrain of both parent and child can help facilitate more compassionate and open conversations as they navigate the road ahead.

A MOMENT TO REFLECT

First, pause here. Take a deep breath before we dig into reflection. Okay. Ready.

How has your relationship with your loved one evolved as they've become more reliant on you?

Are there moments of tension, resistance, or emotional strain similar to those described in the chapter? How do you manage these dynamics?

Reflect on how you manage your emotional response to this role reversal. Have you experienced feelings of guilt, sadness, or frustration as you step into a caregiving role?

How would recognizing this era as the "Adolescence of Aging" help you approach these challenges differently?

CHAPTER 4

Navigating Cognitive Decline and Aging Challenges

"I am beginning to notice that my dad keeps telling me the same thing or asking me the same question repeatedly. He gets upset when I remind him that he has already told me that story or asked that question multiple times. I wonder what's happening." Dad of four, age 57

"Last time when I was with my mom, she walked away from the kitchen to watch the news and left the stovetop burner on, but she didn't realize she did it. She got angry when I asked her about it – she told me to mind my own business." Single, age 45

"When I went to my mom's house, I noticed something on her door. It was a notice of an unpaid, very overdue bill. When I went to her desk, where she keeps her bills, I noticed a large pile of unopened mail. This is so unlike her. I wonder what is going on." Mom of four, age 55

Many people's physical and cognitive abilities deteriorate gradually as they age. For others, this involves the start of dementia, defined by a decline in memory, thinking, behavior, and ability to do daily tasks. Dementia frequently begins subtly, with early symptoms including deficits in executive functioning and effects on the frontal lobe. These changes profoundly impact how aging parents interact with their surroundings and caregivers, often worsening existing tensions in the Adolescence of Aging.

The frontal lobe is responsible for executive activities such as problem-solving, planning, reasoning, and impulse control. When dementia affects this brain area, the individual may struggle to follow logic and reason, resulting in unreasonable or impulsive behavior. These shifts can be perplexing and difficult for adult children functioning as caretakers, especially as they try to balance respecting their parents' autonomy and ensuring their safety and well-being.

Executive functioning refers to a range of cognitive processes required for mental control over behavior. These processes include attentional control, cognitive inhibition, inhibitory control, working memory, and cognitive flexibility, all required for self-management and resource management to attain a goal. When executive functioning weakens, it becomes more difficult for people to handle everyday chores, make decisions, and interact socially in expected ways.

Declines in executive functioning in dementia frequently emerge as difficulty with planning, organizing, and problem-solving. For example, an elderly parent may find it challenging to follow multi-step instructions, regularly misplace goods, or become quickly overwhelmed by decisions that were formerly simple. These cognitive alterations can also impair emotional regulation, increasing anger, mood swings, or indifference.

As dementia progresses, these deficits in executive functioning worsen, making it more difficult for the individual to maintain independence. This transition can be especially difficult for aging parents who, despite acknowledging their limitations, may reject accepting aid to preserve their autonomy.

Dementia-related declines and the Adolescence of Aging can lead to increased friction between aging parents and their adult offspring. In the early stages of dementia, when the individual is still aware of their cognitive decline, they may feel frustrated, afraid, or even in denial about their illness. These emotions might appear in various ways, such as stubbornness, irritation, or aversion to care.

Adult children may experience emotional distress because of their parents' cognitive impairment. The parent-child connection, which traditionally involves the parent providing direction and support, is changing. A mature child must accept more responsibilities, frequently against their parents' wishes. This role reversal can result in guilt, resentment, and helplessness.

Executive Functioning Decline

Keep in mind that the decline in executive functioning can complicate communication. An aging parent with early-stage dementia might struggle to follow conversations or instructions, leading to misunderstandings. They might not remember important details, repeat themselves, or become confused about time and place. These cognitive lapses can create friction, particularly if the adult child becomes impatient or fails to recognize the underlying neurological cause of these behaviors.

Decision-making is another critical issue that arises when executive functioning declines, which is a challenge. Decision-making requires weighing options, considering consequences, and choosing the best action. When these abilities are impaired, the aging parent may make decisions that seem illogical or unsafe, such as neglecting to pay bills, driving despite no longer being able to do so safely, or refusing medical care.

This decline in decision-making ability can be particularly distressing for the aging parent and their adult children. For the parent, the loss of autonomy in decision-making can feel like a loss of self. They may cling to their independence, even when it is no longer safe or practical. This can lead to conflicts with their children, who may feel compelled to step in and decide on their behalf.

The balance between maintaining the aging parent's dignity and ensuring their safety becomes a delicate dance. Supporting an aging parent must navigate this complex terrain with empathy and patience, recognizing that the parent's resistance is often rooted in a fear of losing control over their life. Strategies such as involving the parent in decisions as much as possible, simplifying choices, and offering reassurance can help to mitigate some of these tensions.

Dementia-related declines in executive functioning can lead to significant changes in behavior and emotional responses. The frontal lobe's role in impulse control means that when this area is affected, individuals may become more impulsive or less able to regulate their emotions. This can result in outbursts of anger, sudden mood swings, or inappropriate social behavior, which can be difficult for caregivers to manage.

These behavioral changes can strain relationships, as caregivers may feel hurt, confused, or overwhelmed by the aging parent's actions. Understanding that these behaviors are symptoms of the disease, not intentional acts of defiance or hostility, helps reduce frustration and enables a more compassionate approach to care.

Anxiety is another typical emotional response in individuals with declining executive functioning. As the individual becomes increasingly aware of their cognitive decline, they may worry about the future, fear becoming a burden, or feel anxious about their ability to manage daily tasks. This anxiety can exacerbate behavioral symptoms, leading to increased irritability or withdrawal.

Providing a calm and supportive environment, offering reassurance, and being patient is helpful when the aging parent struggles to express themselves or follow conversations.

Maintaining a routine is also beneficial, as predictability can help reduce anxiety and make the individual feel more secure.

As dementia progresses and executive functioning declines further, navigating the healthcare system and addressing legal considerations become increasingly important. It may require stepping in to manage medical appointments, medications, and finances, often facing resistance from the aging parent. This can be a delicate process involving taking over responsibilities that the parent may still feel capable of handling.

A key legal consideration is establishing power of attorney (POA) for healthcare and financial decisions. This legal document allows a designated individual to make decisions for the person with dementia if they cannot do so themselves. It's crucial to address these issues early in the disease progression while the aging parent can still participate in decision-making.

Obtaining a POA can be fraught with emotional and ethical challenges. Aging parents may resist the idea, feeling that it signals a loss of control or an acknowledgment of their decline. Approach this conversation sensitively, emphasizing the importance of planning for the future to ensure the parent's wishes are respected.

In our experience, other legal considerations include creating a living will, which outlines the parent's wishes for end-of-life care, and making decisions about long-term care options, such as in-home care or assisted living. These discussions can be difficult, but they are essential for ensuring that the aging parent's needs are met in a way that aligns with their values and preferences.

In writing this guide, we are sharing what we have learned from our experience. We are not legal, financial, or mental health professionals; we're not here to give you formal advice.

We are also sharing stories of others who have been on this path and encourage you to know what to expect and what to look for.

We encourage you to contact a professional for any serious concerns or decisions. This is about giving you enough information to help you understand the tools that will help you meet the challenges of caring for your aging parent. This is about finding your helpers and knowing what to ask as you move forward!

Find Your Helpers

Caring for an elderly parent with dementia and diminishing executive functioning is not a solo journey. The role of support networks, which include family, community, and professional assistance, is critical in dealing with the issues that occur.

Family members can provide emotional support and share caring chores. However, caregiving might strain family dynamics. Open communication, clear limits, and mutual support are essential for healthy relationships.

Community resources, such as caregiver support groups and social activities for dementia patients, can be a lifeline. Support groups allow caregivers to share their experiences, learn from others facing similar issues, and receive emotional support. Social activities for elderly parents can help them preserve cognitive function while providing a sense of purpose and connection. Remember, there are resources available to help you.

Professional help, such as home health aides, geriatric care managers, and dementia specialists, can bring caregivers much-needed relief. These professionals can ensure that the aging parent receives proper care and help you manage the behavioral and emotional issues of diminishing executive functioning. Remember, it's okay to ask for help.

One of the most challenging components of caring for an aging parent with deteriorating executive functioning is managing the ethical dimension of caregiving. Balancing respect for the parent's autonomy and guaranteeing their safety necessitates thoughtful analysis and sensitivity.

Respecting autonomy is acknowledging the aging parent's right to make decisions about their life, even if they appear rash or risky. However, when executive functioning deteriorates, the ability to make educated judgments is jeopardized, posing safety and well-being concerns.

This challenge is rooted in many disagreements between elderly parents and their offspring. Caregivers may feel split between respecting their parents' desires and intervening to avert harm. The idea is to approach these circumstances with empathy, understand the parent's point of view, and find ways to involve them in decision-making as much as possible.

Making decisions that go against the parent's intentions may sometimes be necessary, significantly if their safety is jeopardized. This should be done with care, honesty, and a commitment to protecting the parent's dignity. Involving a neutral third party, such as a mediator or geriatric care manager, can assist families in navigating challenging issues and alleviating tensions. Having walked this journey with my family, I can tell you it is not easy, and I had to think long-term. It took years of attentive waiting as my loved one made poor decisions and fell prey to criminals in the realm of financial elder exploitation. It was exhausting to see our existing system used against her.

For more on this subject, visit Amazon and find *The Perfect Pawn: A Senior's Struggle with Financial Elder Abuse.* In this book, I share my story and provide toolkits on how to prevent financial elder abuse, how to respond if a loved one becomes a victim, how to hold a family meeting, and potential changes to make the system safer for vulnerable seniors.

An essential resource for me on my journey and in writing this section is *The 36-Hour Day, A Family Guide to Caring for People Who Have Alzheimer's Disease and Other Dementias* by Nancy

Mace, MA, and Peter Rabins, MD. I recommend this read if cognitive decline is in play for your aging parent.

A MOMENT TO REFLECT

When you're in the squeeze, these changes can feel insurmountable. Let's pause. Close our eyes and take a few cleansing breaths. When you're ready, let's reflect.

What changes in your parent's abilities have you noticed recently that surprised or unsettled you? How did you feel in those moments, and how did you respond?

Reflect on whether understanding these changes as part of the impact of dementia on functioning might shift how you approach future challenges.

When have you struggled with balancing your loved one's desire for independence with your concern for their safety? Think about a recent situation; how did you handle it, and what, if anything, might you do differently next time?

What are some tough decisions that you anticipate facing as your parent's cognitive abilities decline?

Reflect on how you might approach these moments and whether involving a neutral third party or other support might help.

CHAPTER 5

The Emotional Complexity of the Squeeze

The emotional pressure of being pushed in several directions, work, family, personal health, and aging parents—is enormous. As we care for our aging parents, we frequently experience conflicting emotions, such as guilt for not being able to do everything, resentment for the demands placed on us, and a strong sense of responsibility to care for those we love.

Even if your personal life is hectic, there is pressure at work to perform, meet deadlines, and keep a professional demeanor. The emotional burden of caring for children, whether babies requiring constant attention or teenagers negotiating complex life stages, is tremendous at home. Layered on top of this is the obligation of managing the care of aging parents, which presents emotional issues ranging from the pain of seeing a parent's health deteriorate to the frustration of dealing with medical and financial systems.

This ongoing emotional tug-of-war might leave you feeling completely overwhelmed. We feel overburdened with too many obligations and insufficient emotional, mental, or physical resources to satisfy them all. This strain is not only an emotional feeling; it can also emerge as physical symptoms like insomnia, migraines, or chronic worry.

Middle adulthood's mental and emotional weight is complicated and multifaceted. It's not only about task management; it's also about navigating the complex emotional terrain of caregiving, personal health, and preserving some balance in a life that frequently feels everything but balanced. It is difficult to discover ways to manage this load, share it where possible, and realize the enormous strength and resilience required to carry it daily.

The Complex Realities for Women

"After all, Ginger Rogers did everything Fred Astaire did. She just did it backward and in high heels." Ann Richards

"We can do no great things, only small things with great love." Mother Theresa

"If you want something said, ask a man; if you want something done, ask a woman." Margaret Thatcher

Sarah wakes up before dawn every morning, her mind racing through the day ahead. As a senior executive at a high-performance tech company, she's accustomed to her job's fast pace and high demands. Deadlines, meetings, and the constant pressure to innovate are the norm. But lately, it's not just the job weighing on her.

Sarah's two children are deeply involved in competitive sports, requiring frequent travel. Weekends are no longer a time to unwind but are filled with packing, coordinating schedules, and cheering from the sidelines at tournaments in different cities. The car rides are long, and the hotel stays are short, leaving little time for rest.

Adding to her already overflowing plate is the care of her aging parents. Sarah's father was diagnosed with Alzheimer's a year ago, and her mother, who was always the family's rock, is now struggling with her health issues. Sarah constantly toggles between managing care plans, scheduling doctor appointments, and ensuring her parents' safety and well-being. Every day brings new challenges, another health crisis, a complex decision, and another layer of responsibility.

And then, there are her battles. In the quiet moments, when the house is still, and her mind drifts, Sarah feels the weight of something she can't quite name. Fatigue has become her constant companion, making even the simplest tasks impossible. She's noticed fogginess in her thinking, a mental haze that wasn't there before. Decisions that used to come quickly now feel like monumental hurdles. Emotions that she could once keep in check now bubble to the surface unexpectedly, overwhelming her when she least expects it.

Sarah feels overwhelmed. She's doing everything she can to hold it all together, but there are days when she wonders how much longer she can keep this pace. Her load is immense, yet it's mostly invisible to those around her. At work, she's expected to perform at her peak and to lead with clarity and confidence. At home, she's the anchor, keeping everything running smoothly. But inside, she feels like she's barely holding on.

Now, consider Clara, who, at 45, finds herself in a scenario she never imagined. She had her first child after years of focusing on her career and finally finding stability. As she changed her newborn's diaper, she reminded me she did the same for her aging father just yesterday. The irony isn't lost on her: she is now a mother to both her infant son and her parents.

Clara's days are full of feedings, diaper changes, and soothing cries. But it doesn't end there. She also manages her parents' care, organizing home health visits, sorting out medications, and handling the delicate task of ensuring her father's dignity as she helps him with his most basic needs. The physical and emotional toll is immense.

During all this, Clara, too, is facing perimenopause. The hormonal shifts leave her feeling tired and irritable, her body aching with the relentless demands of both motherhood and caregiving. She struggles to remember simple things—where she left her keys, whether she took the chicken out of the freezer—and finds herself crying in the quiet moments, overwhelmed by the enormity of her responsibilities.

Clara's reality starkly contrasts with the serene, older mother she once imagined. She feels like she's parenting two generations at once, caring for a baby who needs her every moment and parents who, in their vulnerability, need her just as much. The question she faces daily is, "How can I be the mother my child needs while also being the caregiver my parents require?"

These two women, Sarah and Clara, are living examples of the intense and complex realities many face in this stage of life. They are the silent struggle of so many women in this stage of life—squeezed between the demands of their careers, raising children, managing the care of aging parents, and navigating the physical and emotional shifts of perimenopause. Theirs is a story of resilience and overwhelming strain—of being asked to do more than one person reasonably can.

As women enter their midlife, a subtle but fundamental transformation in identity begins to emerge. For decades, many women have accepted the job of primary caregiver, the person who nurtures, organizes, and keeps the family together. This identification has frequently been very satisfying, offering a sense of purpose and connection. However, when children grow older, elderly parents require more care, and the realities of bodily changes become apparent; many women experience an identity transition that may be both bewildering and transformative.

Gail Sheehy, a journalist and author of *Passages: A Transforming Guide to the Common Journey of Adult Growth*, describes middle adulthood as a time when people frequently reconsider their roles and identities. Family dynamics, personal aspirations, and the physical changes accompanying aging typically trigger women to reevaluate. Children who once required constant supervision become more independent, occasionally leaving home for college, or beginning their own families. Simultaneously, aged parents who were previously pillars of strength now rely on their daughters for assistance and care. This role reversal can be unsettling, causing women to reconsider their place within the family structure.

Women who have spent years as primary caretakers may wonder, "Who am I if I am no longer required in the same way?" This can lead to a reassessment of priorities, a search for new meaning, and, in many cases, a desire to remake oneself outside their caring obligations.

The identity shift might be much more difficult for those still raising toddlers, teenagers, or elementary school students. The duties of raising young children might make it challenging to find time for self-reflection and personal growth. Juggling schedules, homework, and extracurricular activities gives little time to pursue new hobbies or ponder job alternatives. However, the urge to adapt and change persists as these women balance the demands of raising children and caring for aging parents.

As if these emotional and psychological obligations weren't enough, the physical changes associated with perimenopause and menopause add to the complexities of middle life. The average age of a mother having her first birth in the United

States has consistently increased over the last decade. According to the Centers for Disease Control and Prevention, the average woman will give birth for the first time in 2021 at 27.3. This increased from 2011, when the average mother was 25.6 years old when she gave birth to her first child. (Source: Pew Research Center. Katherine Schaeffer and Carolina Aragao, "Key Facts about Moms in the United States," May 9, 2023.)

Another layer to this discourse is that the hormonal alterations that follow these life stages can cause a variety of symptoms, including exhaustion, hot flashes, mood swings, and cognitive impairments, all of which can impair a woman's ability to manage her duties and preserve her sense of identity. According to the World Health Organization, most women go through menopause between the ages of 45 and 55 as part of the natural aging process.

What no one discusses is perimenopause, which is the earliest warning that your body is likely to enter menopause and can last several years. According to Dr. Mary Clare Haver, an OBGYN expert on menopause, 90% of women over the age of 45 are either perimenopausal, menopausal, or post-menopausal. Perimenopause can have an impact on one's physical, emotional, mental, and social health. (Source: World Health Organization, "Menopause," October 16, 2024.) We are not only caring for our elderly parents, but we are also undergoing significant physical changes.

Energy levels formerly sustained by late nights with infants or marathon workdays may dwindle, leaving women exhausted and less capable of completing their daily chores. Emotional stability, once a source of strength, can become unpredictable, causing mood swings that make managing relationships at home and work more difficult. The mental fog that sometimes comes with menopause can make it difficult to think correctly, adding to an already stressful life.

These physical realities are more than just biological happenings; they are inextricably linked to the identity changes that occur during middle age. The body's changes might serve as a reminder that time is passing, causing a rethinking of life's objectives and ambitions. Women may wonder how they want to spend the next stage of their lives, what legacy they want to leave, and how they will combine their goals with the constant responsibilities of family.

However, when many women begin to navigate this complex reworking of their identities, they face an additional significant challenge: caring for elderly parents. Adjusting from being their children's primary caregivers to caring for their parents can be daunting. The mental and physical challenges of managing this additional responsibility frequently collide with the personal development and exploration women in middle adulthood are beginning to pursue. It adds another dimension to their life, leaving them wondering how to keep their identity and well-being while caring for those who once looked after them.

This convergence of life stages—raising children, going through midlife transitions, and taking on the caregiver job for elderly parents—creates a distinct and stressful era of life. Women are frequently left navigating uncharted territory, seeking a new equilibrium in a society where expectations and duties never seem to stop increasing. The challenge is to care for their loved ones while also making time for themselves and redefining who they are in this new and ever-changing chapter of life.

Their Emotional and Mental Load

Gail Sheehy's idea of the "midlife transition" emphasizes how significant changes in personal identity and roles characterize this time. Many women face a never-ending mental checklist of responsibilities as they make this adjustment. This checklist is more than just remembering to pick up groceries or arrange doctor's appointments; it's a cognitive burden that includes caring for elderly parents, managing domestic needs, fulfilling work commitments, and maintaining personal health and well-being.

This mental weight is frequently unnoticeable to others, but it is a constant, running tally in women's minds in their middle years. Every task and obligation adds to this strain, and the weight can be overpowering without enough support or flexibility.

Consider Robin's experience: she is already juggling the responsibilities of late parenthood with the rigors of a high-pressure profession. When you add in the burden of caring for aging parents, the mental strain becomes almost unbearable. She is responsible for making all decisions, from daycare arrangements to planning medical appointments for her parents. The lack of job flexibility exacerbates the dilemma since she needs more room to modify her professional life to meet these personal obligations. The constant juggling exhausts her, pushing her mental and emotional bandwidth to the brink.

For many women, the lack of spousal support adds to the pressure. The absence of a supportive partner can make the mental checklist feel even more heavy, whether owing to a partner's demanding employment, emotional unavailability, or single parenting. Every task that could be shared or delegated falls directly on their shoulders, resulting in a perpetual mental and emotional overload.

The Reality of External Pressures for Women

Career pressures can be daunting at any age. Nonetheless, they become more demanding during middle adulthood, which is frequently characterized by career reappraisal and increased financial responsibilities. Gail Sheehy's views on this life stage indicate how people often reflect on their professional routes, questioning whether they align with their values and long-term aspirations. This is challenging, and the weight of caring for your family and your aging parents needs to be raised as difficult and weighty.

Many women face intense career obligations during this period. High-stress, rigid occupations can lead to a sense of being stuck when the need for financial security competes with the need for work-life balance. Medical expenditures, long-term care, and even house improvements all add to the financial stress of caring for aging parents. The necessity to plan for one's future, including retirement funds and anticipated healthcare bills, adds to the economic strain.

According to the National Alliance for Caregiving and AARP's "Caregiving in the U.S. 2020" report, 60% of family caregivers work, with many working full time. 56% of these family caregivers are women. Balancing family caregiving responsibilities with a career may be highly stressful, especially for individuals in high-demand positions. Furthermore, women family caregivers report an average out-of-pocket expense of $7,000 per year for caregiving-related charges, often in addition to their regular financial commitments, such as retirement savings.

The combination of job commitments and caregiving responsibilities is a unique difficulty. Women may be unable to take time off or reduce their work hours for fear of losing income or professional positions. The pressure to thrive in their careers while caring for others can lead to burnout, in which the constant juggling act exhausts them and leaves them with little time or energy.

According to the "National Alliance for Caregiving and AARP's 2020" report, 23% of caregivers say caregiving has harmed their health. In addition, 66% of working family caregivers report needing to make workplace concessions, such as reducing work hours, taking a leave of absence, or receiving a performance or attendance warning. Among them, 56% of female family caregivers are more likely to feel job-related stress, with 20% expressing substantial financial pressure due to managing work and caregiving duties.

Furthermore, the financial preparation necessary during this period might be intimidating. Women may face the challenges of managing their parents' finances, making tough decisions about long-term care, and maintaining their financial security. This additional level of responsibility can cause anxiety and stress as they attempt to reconcile their immediate financial requirements with long-term planning.

According to NerdWallet's April 2024 "Financially Assisting Aging Parents Report," more than 36% of Americans believe their parents will require financial assistance as they age, but not everyone can afford to help. And more than 55% of Americans are presently supporting or intend to support their parents financially, whether by paying for items, managing their money, or both. (Source: Nerd Wallet 2024, "Financially Assisting Aging Parents Report," April 16, 2024)

In addition to job and financial constraints, women often find themselves under the weight of societal expectations. The norm dictates that women should seamlessly juggle caregiving tasks for their children and aging parents. As women, many of us have been silently working as hard as we can to meet the expectations of society and trying to do it all. This societal pressure can lead to role strain, a feeling of overwhelming pressure to fulfill various roles—caregiver, professional, parent, and partner.

A 2023 National Institutes of Health article, "Women tend to prioritize others and ignore themselves," discusses how women's caregiving obligations might help or hinder diabetic self-management. The researchers discovered that caregiving competed for time, energy, and money with self-management. They were struggling to balance caring and self-management, creating stress, which women perceived as intrinsically unhealthy and hampered self-management of their disease. According to the article, women were responsible for adult family members, love partners, and caring for children. (Source: Diabetic Medicine "We tend to prioritize others and forget ourselves" January 6, 2023)

Women are also expected to supervise their children's extracurricular activities, which can be a significant added burden. This frequently entails juggling a demanding schedule of sports, music classes, and other high-demand activities that necessitate considerable time, energy, and travel. The urge to ensure their children's engagement and success in these activities can contribute to stress, especially when combined with the obligations of caregiving and professional responsibilities.

This role strain is not only an inward sensation but also perpetuated by cultural and societal messaging that praises women who "do it all" without complaining. Maintaining a façade of effortless multitasking can take an emotional toll, leading to feelings of inadequacy and guilt when reality does not match expectations. It's a hefty load that many women bear without recognition or support. There are costs when we, as women, try to do it all.

According to the 2018 BCBS Health Index, caregivers had an average Health Index of 89.6. This score is 2.2 points lower than the benchmark group, indicating a 26% larger impact of physical and behavioral health issues that may impair their overall health.

The Complex Realities for Men

"I see my wife's hours supporting her mother, who lives out of state. She offers suggestions on how my mother-in-law can age in place, but her mom discounts her ideas. I can't tell you how often she falls and ends up in the emergency room, then needs to be hospitalized, and then in a rehabilitation center. It is like a merry-go-round, with each cycle of hospitalization taking hours on the phone plus travel to ensure that my mother-in-law is ok. My wife has three brothers who do not pull their weight. This is a heavy burden on both of us." Husband, age 62

"I am at my wit's end with my parents. They need to downsize or move to a care facility or assisted living. Each time we tour a property or facility, the list of reasons it won't work is endless. I have four siblings

who don't feel the same urgency or choose to deny it." *Dad of three, age 47*

"*I do everything for my parents. While I have several siblings, they are not actively involved. If they help, it is because I made a fuss about getting them to do something. I am not sure why they do not engage in caregiving. It is hard with my full-time job and the responsibilities of my own family.*" *Son, age 58*

"The National Alliance for Caregiving and AARP" reports that around 14.5 million men in the United States care for elderly family members. This accounts for nearly 40% of people caring for their aging parent, a significant increase from prior years. In 1995, only 11% of family caregivers were men.

We know societal conventions influence how men handle caregiving. Despite changing beliefs, there is still a widespread taboo around men in caregiving positions. On the one hand, society encourages men to be involved and supportive. However, they may encounter shame or censure for doing what is usually considered "women's work." There may be a reluctance to fully embrace or identify with the family caregiving role or seek assistance and support when necessary.

These societal taboos and embarrassment that men may experience in caring for family roles exacerbate this dynamic. While societal standards are gradually changing, men who take on family caregiving obligations may confront questioning or judgments and find caring awkward or uncomfortable. Bathing, dressing, and catering to personal needs can be a challenge for them, especially if they have yet to have role models or instructions on navigating these obligations. It can create uneasiness and feelings of confusion or inadequacy.

Men may also feel pressured to conform to traditional conceptions of strength and self-reliance, making it difficult to accept that they are overwhelmed or struggling. The fear of looking weak or vulnerable can hinder individuals from receiving the emotional support and resources required to manage the complexity of caregiving. This isolation can lead to stress and burnout as men attempt to handle these obligations alone, often without the tools necessary or support networks.

Men may also experience a particular role strain, in which they feel torn between professional obligations and caregiving responsibilities. Attempting to fulfill both tasks efficiently might result in burnout and emotional exhaustion. Men may struggle to cope with these responsibilities without sufficient support networks, leaving them feeling overwhelmed and unsupported.

Like women, they may also be at the pinnacle of their careers, working in high-stress, demanding positions that take up much time and energy. Balancing career commitments and caring duties presents a distinct set of problems. Specific employment inflexibility—long hours, frequent travel, and performance pressure that make it difficult for family caregivers to be present and attentive. The conflict between employment and family caregiving can cause men to feel isolated, frustrated, and guilty as they struggle to meet expectations in both areas.

The financial burden of being the primary breadwinner can also exacerbate the situation. Feeling constrained by the pressure to maintain economic stability while caring for aging parents or children. This combined responsibility can cause tremendous stress as they balance the pressures of job success and caring responsibilities.

The combination of these challenges—awkwardness in family caregiving, societal taboos, and high-stress jobs—makes it difficult for men to achieve balance while providing support or care for a loved one. They may feel lonely and alone in their roles. The scarcity of family caregiving tools for men and support groups makes it difficult for men to find the community and advice they require to navigate this complex landscape.

Recognizing men's particular problems in caregiving is critical for building a more balanced and supportive atmosphere. Recognizing the awkwardness, societal taboos, and professional responsibilities they confront allows us to better grasp the challenges of caregiving from a man's viewpoint. Encouraging open conversations about these obstacles and providing focused support and tools can help men navigate the caring landscape more confidently and resiliently.

In a broader sense, cultivating a culture that appreciates and promotes caregiving, regardless of gender, can help reduce some of the stresses that men confront. By questioning established gender stereotypes and providing more flexible work conditions, we can allow men to take on caring responsibilities without fear of societal criticism or professional compromise. A balanced view of family caregiving acknowledges that it is a shared obligation that necessitates understanding, support, and compassion.

A MOMENT TO REFLECT

Whew. That was a lot of information. Let's pause here for a minute before diving into this moment to reflect.

What are the most important roles you are trying to juggle? Think broadly here - consider all your roles from caregiver, parent, professional, partner, and friend, acknowledging the demands of each one.

How do you feel about the balance of these roles? Consider whether specific roles feel harder or more overpowering than others. Are there any places where you feel unsupported or stretched too thinly?

How do you currently share caregiving responsibilities, if at all, with other family members, friends, or professionals? Are you trying to do everything yourself? Can you delegate, ask for help?

How does the description of identity shifts in midlife resonate with you? Reflect on how caregiving, career demands, and physical changes are affecting my sense of self. Can you carve out space to explore personal growth during this phase of life?

CHAPTER 6

The Hardship of Stress

Stress is a big part of caring for our aging parents. How we manage stress and navigate the challenges that keep coming our way factors into how well we experience this journey. It can be the difference between enduring and thriving.

What does your stressor landscape look like? How aware are you of the stressors your dear body is trying to manage? Do you have the coping skills to maintain balance and health? I sure didn't, and to this day, I am adding tools to my self-care toolbox to remain healthy and strong for myself and my immediate family.

Take a quick stress inventory: Grab a piece of paper and list your stressors. Go on—be complete. Take a few minutes and think hard—what are all the stressors you are trying to manage...

Here are some items I bet your list might include:

- Caring for a spouse.
- Caring for your children and grandchildren.
- Living with a person who needs care.
- Caring for someone who needs constant care.

- Feeling alone.
- Feeling frustrated.
- Having money problems.
- Not enough guidance from health care professionals.
- Having no choice about being a caregiver.
- Not having good coping or problem-solving skills.
- Feeling the need to be constantly "on call."
- Lack of boundaries.
- Trying to manage overlapping healthcare issues.
- Lack of medical knowledge to know what to ask.

Here are a few broader areas that might help you think about and explain what you are trying to manage for those whose **aging parents live with them:**

- Lifting, bathing, and assistance with movement are everyday physical demands in caregiving, which can result in strain or injury. Late evenings are spent answering phone calls from aging parents, and early mornings are spent caring for your family and working to support your family.
- Witnessing the decline of an elderly parent's health or cognitive abilities can be emotionally stressful, causing feelings of sadness, loss, frustration, or guilt.
- Caregiving expenses, such as medical bills, home improvements, and lost pay due to time off work, can strain caregivers.

- Balancing caregiving responsibilities with job, family, and personal life can lead to feelings of overwhelm or burnout.
- Caregivers may face social isolation as they devote more time to caregiving chores, which limit opportunities for socializing and maintaining relationships outside of the caregiving position.
- Caregivers frequently experience interrupted sleep patterns due to nocturnal caregiving duties, frequent awakenings, or concern for their loved one's health.
- Neglecting one's health requirements in favor of caring for aging parents might result in caregiver neglect and an increased risk of physical or mental health issues.
- Caregivers may find managing medical appointments complicated and overwhelming, coordinating care with many healthcare providers, and grasping complex medical information.
- Caregivers may suffer role reversal when they take on additional responsibilities and decision-making authority, straining the parent-child connection and causing resentment or dissatisfaction.
- Caregivers frequently have ambiguity about their loved one's prognosis, future care needs, and ability to continue giving care, which causes anxiety and stress about what lies ahead.
- Caregivers may experience anticipatory grief as they see their loved one's declining health or cognitive abilities, as well as grief and loss after their death.

- Dealing with challenging behaviors like anger, agitation, or wandering can be exhausting and emotionally draining for caregivers, especially if they lack the essential assistance and tools to manage these behaviors properly.

- Differences in viewpoint or caregiving practices among family members can cause conflict, tension, and increased stress for caregivers, especially if there is a lack of communication or support from other family members.

- Caregivers may struggle to find time for self-care and rest from their caregiving responsibilities, causing increased stress and burnout.

- Cultural expectations, beliefs, and conventions can influence caregiving dynamics and increase stress for caregivers negotiating these intricacies.

Here are broader areas for those whose **aging parents do not live with them:**

- Coordinating care from a distance can be complex, including arranging transportation to medical appointments, handling funds, and ensuring that the elderly parents' requirements are satisfied despite the lack of physical presence.

- Limited face-to-face connection might create communication hurdles, making it difficult to assess the requirements of aging parents, understand their preferences, and effectively coordinate care.
- Being physically separated from elderly parents can cause heightened worry and anxiety about their well-being, particularly if they have health problems or live alone.
- Caregivers may feel guilty or concerned about not being physically present to care for their aging parents, which can lead to feelings of inadequacy or fear for their parent's health and safety.
- Caregivers living apart from their aging parents may find it difficult to seek help or share caregiving obligations because their local support network may be small.
- Without regular face-to-face connection, caregivers may struggle to assess their aging parents' changing requirements and identify the level of assistance required to guarantee their parents' safety and well-being.
- Long-distance caregiving frequently necessitates navigating complex healthcare systems, handling medical emergencies from afar, and coordinating treatment among various providers, which can be exhausting and frustrating.

- Caregivers may encounter financial hardship due to traveling to see their aging parents, covering care bills, or taking time off work to provide support, contributing to economic stress and uncertainty.

- The emotional toll of long-distance caring, such as emotions of guilt, concern, and powerlessness, can exacerbate emotional distress and negatively affect the caregiver's overall well-being.

- Balancing caregiving responsibilities with work, family, and personal life from a distance can be difficult, resulting in overload and burnout as caregivers try to satisfy competing demands.

- When caregivers are unable to be physically present, they may feel powerless to ensure their aging parents' well-being and care, resulting in irritation, despair, and uncertainty.

- Living far away from our aging parents might lead to isolation due to the time and energy required to care for them. The time needed for travel and communication with others closer to our elderly parents necessitates hours upon hours of phone calls. If your aging parent is aging in place, be prepared because assisting the transition from Interdependence to Dependence raises expectations significantly. Ensuring your aging parents have everything they need to live at home and providing necessary assistance for them is difficult.

Take a pencil/pen and circle all the stressors you are currently experiencing while walking this journey of caring for your aging parent. Seeing and naming all the pieces on your plate, is important, period. I still recall the day when a friend taught me how to better see all the pieces I was trying to manage, unsuccessfully, I should add.

Below is a snapshot of the stressors on my caregiving journey. I need to be honest: I found it overwhelming to read my full list, so I shortened it. No wonder I was so exhausted and functioning at low levels. I would like you to find pieces and name the stressors on your plate.

Here is my abbreviated list of stressors I experienced:

- Interacting with care facility staff to address the needs of aging parents can be challenging. The care facility or rehab center may not return calls. Remember, the turnover at many facilities is very high, the work is demanding, and the pay is low!
- Dozens of phone calls from my aging parents day and night.
- Managing aging parents when there are stepparents and stepchildren.
- Need to fly out of state once a quarter to ensure my aging parent's care.
- Ensuring aging parents have the needed incontinence briefs, pads, and lotions.

- The financial burden of stepping away from your ability to earn income as you are spending hours caring for an aging parent.
- The numerous health crises with multiple ER/hospitalizations, with the bonus when you live out of state.
- Selling your aging parent's home—from inventorying items and liquidating contents to listing them for sale.
- The hours on the phone: trying to schedule or communicate with healthcare staff and then ensuring paperwork is in place so healthcare providers can talk with you.
- The whole Power of Attorney (POA) process, from ensuring my aging parent is willing to have a POA to having the right level of POA, gives you enough authority to do what you need to do. The bottom line is to find a reasonable elder law attorney.
- Don't forget to negotiate with siblings and family members about the role of POA and the duties that you are assuming.
- Trying to get direction from your aging parents on end-of-life measures and then verifying that the care facility has accurate information in the chart. This was a lesson I learned when my aging parent's facility did not have her DNR (do not resuscitate) noted correctly in the chart!

- Ensure the facility is meeting the needs of aging parents as their need for support and assistance shifts. Be prepared, as this can happen without warning. Then, the big question is whether the facility has openings for the right level of care for your aging parent and whether you can afford the additional level of care. BE READY!

- Please know this—the first 90 days of an aging parent in a new facility or new level of care is ridiculously HARD. BE READY.

- All the above while raising teenagers, getting them through high school, and launching young adults. Does any of this sound familiar?

Let's look at your list again. Do you have more items listed than you imagined? Are you surprised by the number of items? Do you have a plan to help you manage all of this?

I had no idea what I was trying to deal with as I was going through the storms and trying to keep my head above water. It wasn't until I wrote this chapter that I could more fully see all I was trying to manage. It is no wonder that I got sick, and many nights, I lay on the couch in a state of pure overwhelm. I was trying my best; it was simply too much.

My lifelines were connecting to a talented counselor and reconnecting with my dear friends. This exercise will help you find language for all you are trying to manage.

Why does this matter? According to a Stress Management Network article, family caregivers are more likely to have health problems than non-caregivers. Two research studies discovered that family caregivers have inferior physical health. These studies assessed self-reported and objective physical health indices, such as stress hormones and medication use. Caregivers may be at higher risk of health problems for various reasons. Psychological strain may cause or worsen physiological changes and interfere with good lifestyle choices (e.g., exercise, sleeping well, eating nutritiously).

The impact of providing care for an aging parent on the family caregiver's health is determined by the caregiver's vulnerability, available resources, the interaction of vulnerability factors, and their ability to help their family members. This subject requires additional research to identify the unexpected repercussions of caregiving. Source: Caregivers Stress | UCSF SMN (stressmeasurement.org).

The National Council of Aging (Caregiver Stress: The Impact on Physical Health article from October 2022 at ncoa.org) shares the risk of increased heart attacks for caregivers who may develop conditions that include:

- Depression and anxiety
- A weakened immune system
- Excess weight and obesity

- Chronic diseases like heart disease, cancer, diabetes, or arthritis. Depression and obesity can increase the risk of these diseases.
- Problems with short-term memory or paying attention.

Caring for an aging parent can be a long road. The more aware and honest we can be about our stress, the healthier we can be. To find more tools to help tolerate and manage stress, check out our website, PeopleInTheSqueeze.com, or find our companion Sticky, Tricky and sometimes Icky Toolkit coming soon.

Guilt and Shame

Let's talk about guilt and shame. Could have, should have... in our world, many well-intended people can reinforce their feelings of guilt and shame with these types of comments and suggestions. We often feel guilty thinking we could have or should have done more. Our goal in writing this guide is to, in part, give this experience a name. When we can name it, we can create the space needed for those of us who feel this is isolating and hard and are getting no recognition for caring for our aging parents. Navigating the challenges of providing care and support for your parents AND navigating our world is demanding. We should be able to release all the guilt and shame we have.

Many well-intended people I have talked to over the years have discounted and diminished how hard this path has been on my family. I recall so clearly being in the driveway of my mother's house as we were working to empty its contents and prepare the home for sale. To say this task was monumental is an understatement.

I jumped into my car and took a client call on this day. I was desperately trying to keep all my "life plates" spinning. I had prepared well for this call. I had a pre-call with a colleague. I prayed the client wouldn't see the vast dumpster and mess outside the car as I hit the start button for the video meeting. As my clients appeared on the screen, my mind went blank, like 100% blank! The shame I felt and my guilt for not being able to show up well was immense. I started to tear up. My client immediately noticed I was off my game and asked me what was up and what I needed.

The negative tapes went into overdrive in my head. How did I get here? Why does my work have to suffer? Would I lose this client? Fortunately for me, my clients were so kind. They could see the tears welling in my eyes. How was I? Was I traveling? The client (coincidentally, a woman caring for her elderly parent) affirmed what I was going through with an immediate, "I am sorry this is hard for you. Let's take a moment to collect ourselves." Her empathy melted away the shame and deep sadness I felt.

This interaction is often the exception in the workplace. I have had the incredible fortune to have clients who, once I have shared my circumstances, are supportive and check in with me on how caring for my aging parent is going. It is hard to hear from many others that being able to navigate work while caring for your aging parents is an intersection that needs discussion. This is at the top of my mind in the world of employers seeking retention strategies.

Our world is focused on extending support to families with young children, but the concept of needing flexibility to care for aging parents falls off the radar. When the lack of support came into play for me, the guilt of having to choose and the shame of not always choosing my aging parent compounded my negative, shameful feelings.

I cannot tell you how many times, on this caregiving journey, I have felt guilty about not being able to do what I want to do or not being able to perform at the level that I wanted to perform because I am physically and emotionally exhausted. We must begin to name and honor that sometimes our bodies go into freeze mode—overwhelmed, exhausted, and unable to get off the couch. Please see this—it is normal for our bodies to say enough. I'm done. I need rest right now. Stop ignoring me and let me rest!

I struggled with holding on to the guilt and shame. I happened to be in between counselors at the time. There was a gap between intense caring and giving my time and emotions to my aging parent. I was trying to do it all. I tend to over-function, moving faster when my body is in a state of distress. I was consulting, raising my four children in all their beautiful activities, and volunteering in leadership roles. Again, this was during a period of minimal communication with my aging parent, which was still emotionally challenging yet less physically exhausting.

We were fostering an older black Lab, Tasha, who would not leave my side. She intuitively knew I was suffering. She would lay her precious body on top of mine when I lay on the couch. I felt a cold coming on, and soon, I became sick. I never get sick. I don't have the time! As a mom of four, I don't get sick days. My dear husband came over and said, "Okay, sweetie, it is time for an intervention. I know you take the responsibility of caring for your mom seriously, but honey, you are sick, and we, your family, and others, need you healthy and strong. How can we help you reframe, rethink, and reapproach your strategy in engaging with your mom? You've been sick for three weeks—we need you."

This was a huge wake-up call for me. I was carrying the burden of guilt and shame for so long; it was now impacting my health, something that needed to change. My dear husband encouraged me to see a physician who could assess my needs and create a plan to get me back to health and more normal functioning.

I must fully commit to open, candid, and honest dialogue with my healthcare practitioners. I had been struggling with so many physical and emotional challenges that it felt good to get this off my chest. Saying this, I'd say the response from my healthcare providers was less supportive than expected. Responses like this are challenging times for all of us; many are stressed, which was surprising. Yes, we all have a tough time. From a health perspective, my point or question was, what can I do to ensure I am staying as healthy as possible through this stressful period?

I found it incredibly interesting how a couple of my healthcare providers chimed in to share that they were also caring for their aging parents. It sounded highly challenging for them as they have medical expertise and are thrust into the role of being healthcare leaders by other family members. This role is demanding, often fraught with crises and situations beyond our control.

Many don't seem to have the skills and tools to help support those of us who are trying our best to survive caring for our aging parents. It isn't on the radar unless you walk this path of heavy responsibilities trying to navigate our world. When it is shared, the interventions seem to be stress management focused. With this caregiving journey, I hope we can think more holistically about all the areas of our lives that are impacted by caring for our aging parents.

A MOMENT TO REFLECT

You've done hard work in this chapter, taking an honest look at what you've had to manage and navigate. You may have learned that there is a lot more there than you realized or allowed yourself to recognize.

Let's take a moment now to reflect on how you use this new awareness of all that you are carrying.

In what ways can you better manage the mental load of caring for your aging loved ones and other responsibilities? Think about how you can benefit from setting boundaries, asking for help, or organizing tasks differently to feel more in control.

What support systems—whether personal, professional, or community-based—can you lean on more effectively? Reflect on whether you have reached out for help when needed and how expanding your network of support might ease the burden you are carrying. Where do you feel you need more help or understanding?

How can you better communicate your needs and boundaries to those around you, including family, friends, and healthcare providers? Think about situations where you have felt unsupported and how clear communication could help you navigate these challenges more effectively.

What are the small moments or rituals that will help you find tranquility during chaos? Even during enormous obligations, there may be little moments of joy or peace. Consider whether you are giving yourself enough time to recharge and what new habits or small changes might help you feel more balanced and resilient

CHAPTER 7

Finding Language for the Mental Load

Finding the language to communicate the experience and the emotional toll can be difficult, if not impossible. Having the words to describe this mental burden adequately helps express what is happening. It gives others the ability to understand and connect with the experience. Here are some imaginative terms and ideas to help frame these complexities:

Role Fatigue describes the exhaustion of juggling frequently competing roles. Whether you're a caregiver, a parent, a worker, or a spouse, the continual switching between different identities can cause severe exhaustion that isn't only physical but also mental and emotional. When you're supposed to be everything to everyone, you feel tired. Hochschild and Machung authored the book *The Second Shift: Working Families and the Revolution at Home*, which uses the phrase "role fatigue" to describe balancing work and family duties.

Beyond physical tiredness, emotional burnout indicates a depletion of emotional reserves. It is the outcome of constantly offering emotional care to others—whether aging parents, children, or colleagues—while leaving little time for oneself.

This term refers to the emotional toll when caring for others becomes a full-time job, leaving little time for self-care or rejuvenation. Maslach, C., and Leiter, M. P.'s research *Understanding the Burnout Experience* (World Psychiatry. June 15, 2016: 103-11) takes a comprehensive look at emotional burnout and its consequences.

Multigenerational Stress acknowledges the unique pressure that arises from being caught between the requirements of numerous generations—caring for elderly parents while raising children. This stress is exacerbated by being pulled in multiple directions, attempting to satisfy the demands of the young and the elderly while still managing your own life. Silverstein and Giarrusso examine the challenges of working relationships across generations. *Multigenerational Stress* by Silverstein, M., and Giarrusso, R. (2010). A decade-long study of aging and family life. Journal of Marriage and Family, 72(3): 595–611.

Cognitive Clutter is the overwhelming mental to-do list that never seems to finish. Cognitive clutter refers to the mental space consumed by an unending array of duties, such as remembering doctor's appointments for parents, managing work deadlines, and keeping track of children's schedules. The mental commotion makes it challenging to think clearly or achieve peace of mind. In a Harvard Business Publishing Education essay, author Schiano delves into cognitive clutter and mental workload learning environments. Source: *Give Your Brain a Break—Course Design Tips to Avoid Feeling Overwhelmed.* 5

Questions to Ask Yourself When Planning for a New Semester. Harvard Business Publishing Education.

Invisible Labor refers to the hidden work that frequently goes unrecognized but is necessary for the smooth operation of a household or the care of a family. Whether it's the emotional labor of sustaining family relationships or the cerebral load of planning and organizing, this effort is sometimes overlooked but essential. According to author Gillian B. White, three out of every four hours of labor women perform worldwide is unpaid. She writes on invisible labor and how it affects women's lives. Source: *The Invisible Work That Women Do Around the World.* The Atlantic, December 14, 2015.

Caregiver Guilt refers to the emotional load of feeling as if you are not doing enough, although you are giving your all. It stems from the unrealistic expectations that caretakers frequently place on themselves, such as feeling guilty when they can't be everywhere or do everything for everyone and worried about failing to meet their loved one's needs. The American Association of Retired Persons provides information on caregiver guilt and how to deal with it.

Responsibility Overload describes the overpowering feeling of having too much on your plate. It's the sensation of being stretched too thin, juggling too many chores and responsibilities, which causes chronic tension and a sense of being permanently behind. Juliet Schor discusses workload and responsibility overload in her book *The Overworked American.*

So, what role does language or terminology play in describing our experiences? I believe it is critical to acknowledge, validate, and accept these feelings, as they are common among many people in middle adulthood.

By recognizing these experiences—role exhaustion, emotional burnout, and cognitive clutter, we bring attention to people's often-overlooked challenges. This act of identifying is powerful because it allows people to see their own experiences reflected in others, which reduces the isolation that frequently comes with these issues.

It emphasizes that these feelings are not unique to one person but are part of a collective experience faced by many. The pressures of managing multigenerational responsibilities, balancing work, and family, and navigating the physical changes of midlife are shared across this life stage. Recognizing this commonality can be comforting and empowering.

Encourage the use of this new language in everyday conversations. When people articulate their experiences, they can better seek help, set boundaries, and advocate for themselves. Language becomes a tool for empowerment, allowing individuals to communicate their needs more effectively.

Normalizing the Struggle

We must reaffirm that struggling with these issues is a normal part of this life stage. There's no shame in feeling overwhelmed by the demands of middle adulthood. By normalizing these experiences, we can reduce the stigma and encourage more open, honest discussions about the realities of this stage of life.

Recognizing and naming these complexities is not just about understanding the challenges; it's the first step toward managing them. By acknowledging the weight of the mental load, individuals can begin to explore strategies for coping, setting boundaries, and finding support. It's about moving from feeling overwhelmed to feeling in control.

We create a space for individuals to feel seen, understood, and supported by providing language for these experiences and validating the complexities of the mental load. This acknowledgment is comforting and essential to the journey toward finding balance and resilience.

By incorporating these specific challenges into the chapter, you provide a comprehensive view of the multifaceted nature of middle adulthood. This approach helps readers see their experiences in a broader context and prepares them for practical strategies in subsequent chapters.

As you reach the end of this chapter, this is an opportunity to take a moment to step back and reflect on the layers of complexity you are managing in your own life. The challenges outlined here are not just theoretical; they are authentic, lived experiences that many of us face daily. Make and take the time to sit and reflect and see how you feel and what is catching your attention in terms of your current situation with your aging parents. We encourage you to take full advantage of this moment!

Consider the roles you play, your hidden work, and the emotional toll of caring for others while attempting to maintain your well-being. Take a deep breath and allow yourself to recognize the gravity of these duties. You are not alone in this, and acknowledging the entire scale of your situation is the first step in understanding and managing it.

A MOMENT TO REFLECT

Which of the terms or ideas introduced in this chapter—such as role fatigue, emotional burnout, or cognitive clutter—best describes your current experience? Reflect on how this language resonates with your journey caring for aging loved ones and how it might help you articulate your feelings to others.

What hidden or invisible labor am you carrying in your role caring for aging loved ones that often goes unacknowledged? Consider how this work impacts your mental and emotional well-being and whether you can communicate its weight to those around you.

How does caregiver guilt show up in your life, and what expectations are you placing on yourself? Reflect on whether these expectations are realistic and how you might release some of the pressure you feel to "do it all."

How can naming and normalizing your struggles help you connect with others and seek support? Reflect on opportunities to use this language in conversations with friends, family, or support groups to foster understanding and reduce feelings of isolation.

As you reflect on your own experience, appreciate the entire breadth of your obligations, and remember that naming and understanding these problems is a positive start. Recognizing the intricacy of your circumstance is the first step toward regaining control and achieving balance.

The following chapters will walk you through ways of dealing with these complications. They will provide practical tools and insights to help you negotiate the mental load, set boundaries, and seek genuine support. The goal is not merely to survive this stage of life but to thrive in it, finding ways to care for yourself while also caring for others.

You are not alone on this path. Many others have similar issues, and there are steps you can take to live a more balanced and satisfying life. We'll explore these avenues together!

CHAPTER 8

The Storms Hit

Caring for your aging parents often starts with a jarring and disruptive BANG! You can feel like things are out of control and moving quickly. A crisis in your aging parents' physical, emotional, cognitive, or financial well-being is like being underwater, struggling to find solid ground when facing overwhelming circumstances.

For many of us, this stage of life is unnamed and not talked about and hits us like a blind corner. We smash into this phase of life, unprepared and honestly naïve thinking we have the end-of-life plans in place, and my aging parent has a medical team in place; I'm all good. That is until the first storm hits, that moment of a physical, mental, or financial challenge, and then the suffering begins.

We believe countless families are struggling and suffering in silence. Thrust into a space of uncharted waters, and where you have pulled away from your life's challenges (which continue), you quickly become overwhelmed by this new space and find yourself wholly and utterly ill-prepared for this new journey. There is a stunning arrival of the challenges that come your way, coupled with the physical and emotional difficulties that soon place you squarely in the suffering stage.

If you are lucky, you may be able to get your feet back on the ground after the first round of the storm. You may say, "That was hard, but I did it and thank goodness that is over!" You return to your immediate regularly scheduled programming of caring for your family at home, your job, and your life, only to realize that another round of waves of the storm keep coming while your other responsibilities stack up.

And this is the new normal...

In the Midst of the Storms

A dear friend said, "Heather, it's like a storm where the waves keep coming." Our first reaction tends to be panic and unsettled. Or, put more bluntly, it is like being knocked on your bottom, time and time again. And, oh my goodness, when the chaos comes, it comes, and it is stunning. What I didn't tell her is I know the emotional rollercoaster of the storms firsthand. And this is how I'd frame it today—buckle up, buttercup; it is a helluva ride.

Here is how my storm rolled in...

I got a call from my brother saying the police were on the phone with him, asking if we had keys to my parents' home. I could not wrap my head around the words, let alone the actual ask of whether I had a set of keys to my parent's house over 1,000 miles away. I could feel my chest tighten, I could feel my gut ache, I could feel my head trying its best to work. My body's fight, flight or freeze mode was FLARING. I could not think straight, and I had to have my brother repeat the question that was being asked of me at that moment. I had no clue of the challenges that lay ahead.

We gave the police permission to kick down the door. I stood in stunned silence; what can I do? What can I do? My brain allowed itself to have the thought of oh wow, my parent may not even be alive. I kept trying to grasp the seriousness of this situation and account for potential outcomes. I heard the EMTs on the scanner report the patient being transferred to the hospital. Ok I told myself; it looks like my parent is alive.

When storms arrive, feelings of panic and drowning can intensify as the weight of the crisis becomes real. You feel overwhelmed and unsure how to proceed, grappling with a sense of helplessness. In my story, my brain could not process the seriousness of the situation as it unfolded.

From my graduate studies in biopsychology, I know that when our brains are under stress, a part of the brain called the amygdala fires up. When this part of the brain fires up, it takes top priority and demands energy and resources from other parts of the brain. This means that when you are under stress, your ability to access and use the thinking part of your brain diminishes greatly. In literature, this is called flipping your lid. Your brain perceives a threat, and survival becomes a top priority. You literally may not be able to engage your thinking brain.

Of course, when you are in storms or crises, you are called upon to make critical decisions under immense stress. This decision-making is often made more complex by resistance from your aging parents and even from nonalignment with family members regarding the next best step. Poor self-care, which often includes poor sleep, diet, and lack of exercise, can compound the situation.

Being able to think, intake complicated information, make sense, negotiate with your aging parent and family members, and solve problems becomes challenging. All these variables are ones that I've seen repeated with frequency in family systems with aging parents. And it comes at a cost—a cost to our aging parents, a cost to our families, and a high cost to us, those who are trying our very best to care for our aging parents. It's like a constant undertow that you can't get ahead of.

If you would like to continue exploring the challenge of stress as we care for our aging parents, you can check out our website, PeopleInTheSqueeze.com, or find our companion Sticky, Tricky and Sometimes Icky Toolkit.

As the needs of my aging parent became apparent, the amount of time in my day spent trying to wrap my arms around the gap between what my aging parent needed to function and her current state became apparent. When you're in a state of trying to assess how bad things are, you lose track of time. You lose track of what day it is, what hour it is, what it is. As I shared before, one night, my dear husband came to me saying, "It was time for an intervention. You have a bad cold, you are not caring for yourself, and we need you."

I was defensive at first, trying to deflect. He helped me see that it wasn't just a couple of days or weeks, but months of me with my head down deep in the weeds of trying to care for my aging parent. I had lost my sparkle, my perspective, and my health.

Isolation and loneliness become a reality as the storms and crises pull you away from your routine. It is impossible to balance work, family, and caring for your aging parent—this undertow of storms and constant caregiving pulls you under and away from so much of what brings you life and joy. With poor self-care, without the joy of your friends and family, your feelings intensify feelings of isolation.

When your parent is in the Adolescence of Aging, clarifying the dynamics in play will give you language and understanding of what tensions you are experiencing. When you reach the point where your parents require more support, they move from a state of self-sufficiency and independence into interdependence. You start to see clues—the beginning of naming those needs for additional support is when the grit first enters the gears.

As I began to name the need for additional support and assistance, I encountered emotionality from my parent, which caused the fall and complete fracture of the relationship. The situation became more and more dire as I tried to work around the challenge. Perhaps my problem was extreme; my relationship with my aging parent was fractured for several years while I worked behind the scenes, tugging and trying to find any solution to provide additional support for my aging parent. I had to make peace with the fact that I would only be able to assist my aging parent when a full crisis hit be it a health crisis or a housing crisis. Only a crisis could create a level of dissatisfaction and urgency needed to ensure healthcare providers and others to see the desperate need for additional supports for my aging parent. I shifted to preparing for when this crisis would come, knowing it would be BIG and GRAND and DRAMATIC, and it was...

The sense of helplessness and frustration with the systems in our society, from our healthcare system to our social support system to the safety net programs for our seniors, did not provide a voice for the adult children of aging parents to fully raise their concerns and find the support and assistance that my aging parent needed. It also opened my eyes to how many elders and their adult children suffer silently. This lit a fire in my belly—how can we improve it for others?

As an adult child, trying to work within this system was brutal. This, coupled with COVID-19, added to the complexity. Ultimately, recognizing this transitional life phase for what it was and giving it a name—the Adolescence of Aging—has finally given me the language and understanding to get to what was really, really going on with my aging parent. It was also stunning how helpful this language has been with many friends and strangers. I am humbled repeatedly at how many of us adult children of aging parents identify with this experience, recognize our parents are in an Adolescence of Aging stage of life, and they may also be suffering in silence.

Transitioning from independence/self-sufficiency to interdependence is a normal part of life that happens to everyone, so we should be able to anticipate these storms. It is in our culture. We have gotten more comfortable with end-of-life and the ability to enter hospice care. We have given this stage of life a name, and well, it is difficult, and some find it impossible to talk about this as a stage that we associate with a normal part of life. But, despite it not being easy, we can all communicate about it because we have given it a name. End-of-life and hospice/palliative care are universally understood stages of life.

The beauty of the Adolescence of Aging life stage construct is that—like the Adolescence of Youth—it is not age-dependent or different. People require different additional supports and assistance at various points in their lives. Having this awareness and eyes wide open that this is on the horizon will help us better see what's coming. We believe it will also ultimately allow for healthier relationships in families and healthier humans.

Understanding this developmental phase of life and having a name for it will give you the roadmap you need as you enter the world of caring for your aging parents. Having language is a game changer and a neutral frame to have conversation and shared understanding of the dynamics in play.

A MOMENT TO REFLECT

Again, let's take a moment here first to breathe. Calm our mind. Calm our bodies. When you're ready, please proceed.

When was the first storm in your experience supporting your aging parent or loved one, and how did it impact you emotionally and practically?

What areas of this experience do you find most overwhelming or challenging?

How do you handle the stress of caring for your loved one during crisis moments? Are there specific strategies that help you remain grounded, or are there new approaches from the chapter that you could try in future situations?

Reflect on the impact this experience has on your health, social life, and personal well-being. Have there been any signs that you may need to re-evaluate your self-care?

CHAPTER 9

Moving from Chaos to Calm

Before diving into this chapter, please take a breath and be ready. Depending on where you are on the journey, you may not like what I will share. If you have picked up this guide to cast blame on your aging parent or others, this may be hard for you. If you are so mad, you cannot see straight it's likely because you did not sign up for this. You might be angry because this chaos is at your front door, and you want no part. Well, here is the deal: regardless of how you got here, regardless of your current state of being and chaos, to get through this storm and over to the other shore in one piece, we are going to ask you to do something that you may want to resist—are you ready?

The hardest part of creating positive change in this is **accepting that we, the adult children of aging parents, are the ones who need to change**.

You didn't choose this. This is happening to you. Why should I have to change?!?! Well, it is because you have the capacity and the ability to consider and own your reaction and response to what is happening. You have a choice. You can choose to stay mad. You can choose to be defiant and oppositional, maybe even choosing to mirror the behavior of your aging parents. That is an option. And it is ok to say, nope, this is too soon. If so, maybe put down this guide and come back to it in six months if your current approach is not working for you.

But if you're curious, this might save you the time and heartache that so many have endured before. We believe that navigating this stage of life can be better.

Our loved ones are in this transitory period of decline: the Adolescence of Aging. They are experiencing the world differently now. Their ability to show up in their world has changed—and not always for the better. They cannot do the things they want to do or be the people they are used to being. It is frustrating, painful, and challenging for them.

If you have raised a child through adolescence or youth, you already know that power struggles never lead to good outcomes. You certainly can never take things personally. And 100% of the time, you are blamed for something that is not really your problem or even your fault, but here we are. Words are often used as weapons and let me tell you, it's a helluva roller coaster. So, buckle up buttercup, here we go into the PITS – People in the Squeeze!

Our baseline response is to fight or retreat from battle.......

Returning to our higher selves, we hold steady as the calm in the storm.

This is what it is like to parent our parents through the Adolescence of Aging. We can develop a new set of muscles and learn to be calm in the storms, anticipate, and know what is around the corner as our parents age. A critical muscle we need to develop is self-control and restraint. The ability to bite our tongues, not escalate, and extend grace goes against our inner self that might be screaming from the mountaintops.

Hear this, maybe read this twice- **WE HEAR YOU. We know how hard this is. We are in the same squeeze and sometimes pinch as you are.** We hope you will begin to see the patterns of behavior and the triggers for your aging parents, and you will develop this new superpower: TO BE CALM IN THE STORM.

Our hope is that you will anticipate the chaos and know what is next. You'll learn to ask questions like DO YOU WANT ME TO LISTEN? OR DO YOU WANT ME TO HELP? You'll learn to affirm the emotion and immediately know how to switch the topic. These strategies are life savers, and we are excited to share them with you.

A New Way Forward

Caring for your aging parent is outside of your control. You will have a lovely morning, a relaxing evening, or a calm hike in nature, and then, out of nowhere, from around the blind corner, comes a storm you had no idea was coming.

I suffered and learned to endure. In talking with friends, I knew they were in the same space: gut it out and persevere at all costs. This is what it is. I want better for you.

The storm was extraordinarily long for me, and I found that the waves associated with this storm just kept coming. I am writing a memoir, The Perfect Pawn: A Senior's Struggle with Financial Elder Abuse, with the lessons I learned on this journey of hardship. Each wave and round of challenges made me more isolated, exhausted, and overwhelmed. It is out of that memoir that the concept of a model or—a transformation that I underwent—to navigate better the challenges associated with caring for my aging parent.

It wasn't until I witnessed my co-researcher, Jayne, struggle with her aging parents-in-law that the depth of my sadness fully surfaced. It wasn't until I saw the sacrifices and hardship impact her life that I was so sad and more fired up than I expected. I know this about myself, I get more motivated when I am mad! My WHY was solidified.

In these moments of hardship and chaos, I want you to place your feet firmly on the ground. Tap your feet on the ground. Take some deep breaths. Sit still for at least a moment and allow yourself to be present. You will need to learn how to find still and pause during chaos.

You can use this technique in the emergency room or as you sit on hold for literally hours trying to navigate care for your aging parent. Trust me, you can learn to find the pause in the storm. You have the strength and resilience within you to weather this storm. Keep reading for your first steps.

Countless others are navigating their storms, caring for their loved ones. We are all on this journey together, yet often, we are unable to see or acknowledge the suffering of others.

I want you to know I understand and support you on this journey. I encourage you to lift your head, see that glimmer of hope, and know that there is a path to follow. By daring to find hope in the darkness, you can begin to find the strength and resources you need to continue moving forward on this journey.

The following chapters offer a simple way to navigate and survive while caring for your aging parents. This process includes Pausing, Assessing, Choosing, and Embracing. Each step is designed to help you manage the challenges and find moments of peace and joy in the storm.

When you PACE yourself at the start of a storm, you give yourself a new set of muscles to respond to whatever comes your way. You are empowered. You develop new strategies that give you inner calm and control to navigate and eventually change how you react to the challenges of caring for your aging parents.

It is a lifeline to move forward. It provides a manageable path— a new way forward with tools and skills to choose and regain your power. We hope this will give you what you need to chart a better path forward for both you and your aging parent! And it will provide you with hope.

A MOMENT TO REFLECT

Think about what calm looks like for you. **How do you define calm in this season?**

It's different for everyone, so imagine, just for a moment, **what would change if you could shift from chaos to calm?** Would it bring you clarity, a softer approach, or a bit more patience?

What's the one thing you can carry with you to invite more calm into your journey?

CHAPTER 10

Charting a New Path

A dear friend told me that whatever you're going through, add a comma to the end of it and "for now." This strategy has gotten me through some challenging moments as a parent and the one caring for an aging parent. This is hard, grueling work FOR NOW. I am struggling with caring for my aging parent FOR NOW. Selling my parent's home is hard FOR NOW. Whatever it is, please know this is not forever; it's hard FOR NOW."

The PACE model will be a resource you can call on as you enter the world of caring for your aging parents. In the storm with its undertows and all the demands spinning around you, countless others are caught up in their storm, caring for their loved ones.

How do we stop the craziness of these storms?! I have learned that while we cannot prevent the storms that come with our parents' aging, we can be better prepared knowing that a transition is on the horizon. As our parents age and need additional support and assistance, we can expect a transition. We can PACE ourselves.

First, PAUSE. It begins by discovering the power of pause. Pausing allows you to separate yourself from the storm. Gather your senses. Calm your mind and body. And most importantly, it will enable you to breathe. It may only be for a few seconds, but you become aware of the churn at that moment. You can see what is happening around you. And, in that moment, you are an island. In the PAUSE, we learn to see better the storms that churn around us as we care for aging parents. We permit ourselves just a moment to take a deep breath. Finding your strategies that allow you to PAUSE in chaos is critical. This might be breathing, tapping, singing, laughing, or moving your body. You might excuse yourself to get a drink of water. Or it could be that you need to use the restroom or tell your parents that you forgot something in the car. Whatever you need to do to step out of chaos, find your quiet and pause.

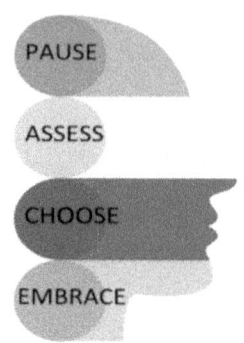

An excellent place to start is to ask how you will know when to pause and what clues your body will give you. While each person's response to the stress or chaos of the moment will trigger different reactions, I'd like to share with you what I know about the Vagus nerve.

As we have mentioned in the chapter about stress, your body will give you physical clues: heavier breathing, tightened chest, headaches, and digestive issues. This is the Vagus nerve. This nerve acts as a bridge between your brain and your body and plays a crucial role in your body's ability to manage stress. It runs from your brain through your chest and into your gut. And guess what? The vagal response can look like bad headaches (this is a migraine for me), panic attacks (like increased heart rate and heavier breathing), and digestive issues with your gut.

All these actions by the body prepare you for fight or flight. And let us remember the last piece of this is FREEZE. Many times, when we get into a stress response, our body can stop, literally freeze. I sometimes need to stop, find a couch, and lie down when overwhelmed. My body needs time and space to settle before I can jump back into action—this is normal!

Pausing in the moment, you begin to feel that these clues from your body are a new muscle that will help you when the storms hit. It will get you out of the reactionary lizard brain and get back into the thinking brain. This takes practice, and we realize that even the most seasoned among us—when we are tired, hungry, and alone—can easily get pulled back into the STORMS that churn around us. Give yourself grace and space to acknowledge that this muscle is complex and will require practice to master the power of pause.

For instance, I once flew east to check in and see how Mom was doing. It was a long day of travel, and I had finished visiting with her and seeing my other family in town. I was an hour or so into my niece's volleyball game when I got a call from my parent's facility that she had fallen in the shower and was going to be sent on her own in an ambulance to the emergency room. Knowing my mom's level of functioning, imagining her by herself in an emergency room in the late afternoon and evening was stunning to me. I immediately offered to go to the facility, pick her up, and take her to the emergency room. I'll never forget being in that waiting room and seeing five other women my age with their aging parents. Five of us out of the twenty people in the waiting room were there with their aging parents.

Because I had spent the day traveling, my phone battery was at zero. I had not eaten lunch or dinner, and I knew it would be hours before the staff saw my mom. Trying to keep her calm, trying to keep her from standing up and walking around, trying to stall until the staff could see her, was challenging. After we checked in with the staff and she was taken back, I offered to go with her, and the nurse looked at me dead in the eyes and said if we need you, we will get you. I laughed out loud, thinking they have no idea about her needs and her sundowners. Well, this should be interesting. The small window made me decide to step outside and find a break in this storm.

I was overwhelmed by all the noises, smells, and thoughts of what needed to come next. I stepped outside the emergency room's chaos, taking deep breaths of fresh evening air and looking at the stars in the night sky. That night, I made videos in the ER parking lot to capture and share how I had learned to PAUSE amid chaos.

Taking breaks and finding windows of opportunity to find peace amid the storms is a critical muscle that I have learned to develop. Practicing these steps and learning what works for you is important in growing and powering up as you navigate the challenges of caring for your aging parent.

I'd love to share another story with you, which I now find humorous.

As I've mentioned before, my aging parent was a victim of financial elder abuse, which meant I needed to advocate for her with different agencies, including the Internal Revenue Service. She needed to appear with an IRS agent in person as we tried to negotiate substantial fines, penalties, and interest. I wanted the IRS agent to see her current functioning state, so we made an appointment to see this agent. Luckily, I asked my brother to join us as I had no idea what it would be like to take my aging parent through security and to a federal building. And I am so glad that I did.

Going through the IRS security was more intense than getting through airport security. My brother and I had our hands full trying to get my aging parent through the levels of security. Five minutes into the meeting with the IRS agent, it was clear to him about the challenges we were trying to negotiate, and he was compassionate and supportive in coming up with a resolution. Minutes into our meeting, my aging parent stated she had to use the restroom, and my brother kindly offered to take her.

Upon his return, his face was flushed, and he had a look in his eye that I knew something was up. He leaned over to whisper in my ear that my aging parent had brought her four-inch knife with her in her walker, and we were in a secure building with a weapon. With all the pressure of what was riding on this meeting, we needed to devise a resolution. And now my aging parent has a steak knife, an actual weapon in her walker. How the hell did it get through the security screening?

My heart was pounding; I was trying to keep my cool and thought I would lose it. But then I thought, wait a hot second. I can do this. I have new PAUSE muscles and could laugh and take a deep breath instead. I tapped my feet and told myself, you are here with your brother. You can do this. And do you know what, we did it—together. Steak knife and all.

I've learned from my counselor that laughter is the best medicine. It helps you to take deep breaths; it lifts the seriousness of the situation and gives your brain a break. One of the key reasons we've decided to knit humor into our work is the power of laughter. I keep several funny memes and videos nearby, so I know I can go to them in those challenging moments, and they will bring a smile to my face. I also know I have several girlfriends who can help me find humor in any situation. Learning PAUSE is critical to surviving the storms!

A MOMENT TO REFLECT ON PAUSE

Take a moment and think about a recent storm you experienced with your aging parent, and consider these reflective questions:

1. **Do you see a moment** when pausing might have changed the course or outcome of the storm?

2. **Which "pause" strategies** make sense? What might they look like for you?

3. **Can you identify** their internal cues and triggers that will tell you when you know they need to pause, i.e., they feel their heart racing or a pressure headache?

Then ASSESS. After you have taken a moment to pause and have calmed your body, your mind is ready to ASSESS the situation. This stage allows you to ask critical questions to help you escape the chaos and better explore your options. Guided by a few fundamental questions, you can better understand the problem, identify patterns, and make informed decisions.

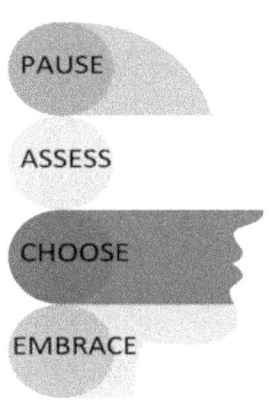

PAUSE

ASSESS

CHOOSE

EMBRACE

Being in the right mindset to evaluate your situation and options is critical. Many times, what is happening is beyond our control. The key to our mental and physical health is being prepared with options for how we might respond. My counselor told me, "Heather, you must see yourself as a repairperson. You may not know what lies around the corner, but you know you have a toolbox of responses ready to pull out whatever tool you need to respond." I have learned, with much practice, that I can control how I respond to whatever chaos comes my way. This helps us get to the root of diffusing stress. We can let go of the need for control, knowing we are prepared with our toolbox to respond to whatever comes to our front door.

When faced with a storm, here are some questions I try to keep in front of me. They help me understand what's going on and guide my next steps.

- What is really, really going on?
- Is this a behavior that I've seen before with my aging parents?
- Is this a new crisis or behavior pattern?
- If this is the same pattern of behavior, what's different?
- What do I need to move forward and remain healthy?

Lastly, as we prepare to move to the next phase, who can help?

In this new place, you can consider your needs. This is a significant pivot as it reframes what you need and what you are missing to move forward. It is giving it a name and realizing that you're struggling and need support.

Now that you have language and can articulate your needs, you may also find that you are able to express your feelings. In doing so, you may discover a pattern of needs resulting from the additional burden of caring for your aging parents. You cannot do it all, but it feels familiar, as you have been here before. Now that you are armed with language to express your needs, you have what you need to seek support.

This may be a new place for you, but being able to reach out to others for support and validation will help you realize that you're not alone in your struggles.

 Remember, finding a community of fellow caregivers is not a sign of weakness but a testament to your strength and resilience. It's a step toward finding the support and understanding you need.

As you gradually share your burden with friends and family, you will find solace and support in their empathy and understanding. Discovering a community of fellow caregivers offers a glimmer of hope and affirmation amid chaos.

You can use your new resources to connect or reconnect with your community. Rather than feeling untethered and unanchored, you are starting to find your sea legs and trust that there is a way to navigate this storm differently. Now, you step into the next stage, which is choosing.

As the storm continues in caring for your aging parents, you can respond better to versus react to what comes next. You are realizing what you can and what you cannot control. You are quicker to bounce back from when the waves knock you over, or better yet, can you withstand the waves as perhaps they move around you?

A MOMENT TO REFLECT ON ASSESS

Take a moment and think about a recent storm you experienced with your aging parent, and consider these reflective questions:

1. **Do you see a moment** when assessing the situation that might have changed the course or outcome of the storm?

2. **Which "assess" strategies** make sense? What might they look like to you?

3. **Can you identify** the resources and network of helpers available to them when they need them?

You CHOOSE. You have paused to calm your body. You've assessed the situation and identified your options and needs to move forward. CHOOSING how to proceed is the TURNING POINT in the model. This is the defining moment for you. This is the game changer—having a choice is what this moment is about.

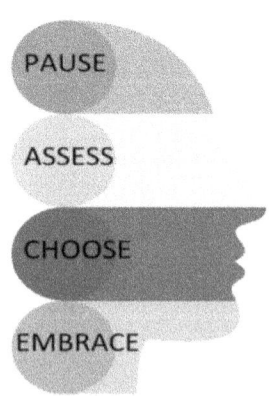

Within this calm and mindful problem assessment, the choice is about empowerment AND action. The shift within you helps you tame the storms and it's empowerment knowing that each storm may require different responses and actions from you. As the storms keep coming, your ability to navigate and get through them is the shift. This is the place to work the PACE Model.

We want you to start to feel a lightness in your experience, a glimmer of hope. We have an opportunity here to bring it to life through personal stories.

Another gift of being able to PAUSE during the storm is that you can have a new perspective as you go through it. Dang, one of the first storms I encountered with my aging parent was when there was a health crisis, and the social worker made judgments that were way off base. Rather than responding defensively or accelerating an already tense situation, I could take deep breaths and gather myself to say she has no idea of the situation and is "shoulding" on me. I could see that the social worker couldn't PAUSE, was stressed, and was not at her best.

This inflection point emphasizes the significance of conscious choice and agency while supporting an aging parent, highlighting the transformative potential of choosing a new perspective. This is where you are more aware of what is happening around you. Now you can better see the dynamics of the whole playing field. You can better evaluate and ask yourself what is happening, and now you know you have a choice in how you will respond. You are empowered, and your ability to be healthier in a more responsive space and mindset is critical for this phase.

As you navigate the tumultuous seas of providing care, you reach an inflection point—a moment of reckoning where you must decide whether to fall back into familiar patterns of overwhelm and despair or forge a new path of resilience and adaptability. This pivotal moment, this ability to choose, shapes the trajectory of your journey, marking a turning point toward empowerment and growth.

A MOMENT TO REFLECT ON CHOOSE

Take a moment, as this truly is an inflection point, to begin naming how you would like to "choose" in future storms.

1. **Give language** to your current experience in the storms. Describe it as if you were telling a friend about it.

2. **What do you want** your storm experience to be like? Complete this statement: I choose...

3. **Write several "Choose" statements** that share how you want to experience future storms.

Finally EMBRACE. You have chosen how to move through storms even as they continue to roll in. You have redefined your relationship with the storms. By doing so, you EMBRACE a mindset that represents a conscious decision to embrace a new perspective and approach, navigating the challenges with resilience and creativity rather than succumbing to despair.

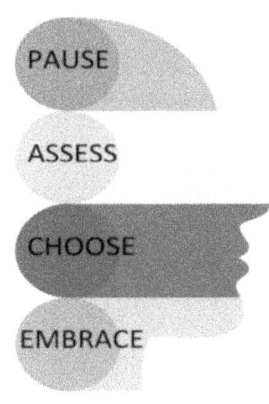

Faced with adversity, you reach a pivotal moment of choice—to resign yourself to the storm's fury or to dance in the rain, finding strength and resilience in the chaos. It's a transformative decision, beginning a journey toward empowerment and self-discovery.

In this stage, you harness support networks and personal resources to regain solid footing, empowering yourself to face challenges with resilience and adaptability.

Drawing strength from your support network and personal resources, you reclaim firm ground beneath your feet. Empowered by newfound resilience, you confront challenges with renewed purpose and determination.

Now, you can begin to find healing. You are moving from suffering to endurance, fostering personal growth, healing relationships, and finding peace in the ongoing challenges.

Transitioning from our initial suffering and chaos to learning skills that help you manage the storms, you can heal and become whole again. Relationships strained by caregiving begin to mend, and in the ongoing challenges, you are now able to find peace while caring for your aging parents.

My journey has been a long one. For me to stand here, where I know that the storms will continue to come, that I may be in the eye of the storm in terms of what lies ahead for me, but this is different; I am different. Now, when the storms hit, I have the muscles to see them and not get wrapped up and pulled into them. It is almost like I can admire the storm if that makes sense. I can be more fully present, and I can better support my aging parent as they suffer and struggle in the storm. I can offer my assistance, love, and support while keeping myself in a more neutral state. I can find my pause, assess, and ask questions of myself and those supporting my aging parent, and then choose how I engage and respond. These shifts are monumental for me. Possessing the muscles to get through the suffering and enduring and finding a place where I can choose how I will be during the chaos is so significant.

What remains a challenge for me is the healing. I can sense in my body that I am still in a state of fight or flight. For eight long years, I wrestled this demon and unnamed life stage, and it has taken a toll on my body. I see myself actively in the embrace-it space. I am learning how to move forward where I can heal and repair the places in my life that I have suffered because of this jealous and demanding place of caring for an aging parent.

This past spring, for the first time in my life, I attended a Silence Retreat at an incredible center for healing in Minnesota. Never in my life have I been quiet for more than five minutes, let alone for an entire weekend. Being able to be in a place where I can step away from caring for my aging parent and trusting the facility is a vast, and I mean tremendous, gift to me. What was I going to do for a quiet weekend?

Let me tell you, being able to settle takes a lot of work. My ears were ringing, and my thoughts raced around: Was my parent, okay? Was my family, ok? Was I ok? I found myself being called to move my body and explore the grounds. As I mentioned previously, there is such power in movement and processing your emotions. I found myself walking and finding a spot to sit. I had to set a timer to force myself to settle in the places around the property. I tried to ask my heart, mind, and body what it needed to become whole again. I focused on my surroundings and forced myself to be fully present.

Settling into the silence and settling into myself was more complicated than I imagined, but the peace I had been chasing came. I had this beautiful moment in the woods surrounded by tall trees. I began to give the trees names of the challenges I have faced in caring for my aging parent, like—frustration, anger, no one listening to me, no one seeing my need and that of my aging parents; why is this so damn hard, why do adult children need to suffer and endure this unnamed life stage, all the lost time with my children and husband, on and on I was able to name the losses I have suffered.

Sitting with this for several hours, I found a place to let go of what was lost and pivot to what was ahead. With my new muscles in place, how can I better balance caring for my aging parent and the life that I want to live? And goodness, what does that life look like? What are my dreams and hopes? When was the last time I could invest in myself in this way? What healing is needed for me to regain my sparkle, and what are my first steps into this new chapter of caring for an aging parent with the PACE model? I found myself highly encouraged.

As I found this place of peace, I realized I couldn't make a complete loop of the grounds over the Silence Retreat weekend while walking the property. The property has wonderful names for the different spaces where you can, for example, climb to the top of a hill and look ahead in your life or release that which no longer serves you.

Well, there was a bridge that signified me being able to let go of all the suffering and pain that I have experienced over these long years. The weight of suffering and enduring has become heavy. I have put on weight, and my body is screaming for self-care and more awareness of the cost of this burden. Several times over the weekend, I walked right up to the edge of the bridge and said to myself, no, I am not ready to let go of all the hurts, anger, and frustration; I am not prepared.

On the last day of the retreat, I got up early, marched around the loop, and came to the bridge. I went to the closest side, found a stump, and plopped down. I reflected on all those trees in the forest and all the pieces to this complex journey I have been on. I thought about all the other women and men who have come across my path and have shared how they have suffered and endured. And it was at this moment that I was at another level of choosing. What was I going to choose for how I live in the future? Can I step into what is next and move out of this hard, lonely, and isolating space?

I stood up, tapping my feet on the ground to help me focus. I took a deep, deep breath and allowed myself to release years of hurt and suffering. I said, "Okay, girl, get yourself over this bridge into your next chapter." And do you know what? I did it. I marched across that bridge with tears streaming down my face, and I could feel the heaviness lifting off me. I was releasing all this being in the squeeze to the universe.

I was energized as I walked back sniffling and trying to gather myself. I was charged up and encouraged to share this with others. My friends, this is the promised land. My hope for you, dear reader, is that you can better see what you are facing, that you can find language, and that you, too, can feel it is possible to move from suffering and enduring chaos to a place of calm and peace where you can smile and thrive. Most important to me is that you know it is possible.

A Moment to Reflect on EMBRACE

Take a moment to reflect on what your "embrace" looks like:

1. **Complete this statement:** I will know I have arrived at the "embrace" when...

2. **How will you feel** when you are able to embrace the storm and this experience?

3. **As you begin to see the possibility** of making it through this challenging stage of life, caring for your aging parent, can you name how you will make space for healing?

CHAPTER 11

Facing Future Storms

In the seemingly turbulent waters of caring for our elderly parents, we face storms challenging our endurance, resilience, and faith.

From medical crises and financial difficulties to emotional turmoil and spiritual doubt, these stormy seasons threaten to engulf us at every step.

In the eye of the storm, there are moments of unexpected calm—a respite from the chaos and turmoil surrounding us. Whether it is a quiet conversation with a loved one, a moment of prayer or meditation, or a simple act of kindness from a friend or family caregiver, we discover that even during the storm, there is peace to be found. But this moment of calm can also be misleading and trap us in a cycle of storms.

One of the critical muscles we hope you will develop by PACE-ing through each storm is a sense of freedom, like you could dance in the rain. Some storms can be tsunamis. If you face wave after wave after wave of crisis—you need to develop another muscle—the ability to float.

As a young girl, we would spend summers on the East Coast of Florida. I learned at an early age all about rip tides. When a rip tide happens, you must fight the urge to swim you must surrender to the current, and float it out. There have been several cases when the storms were overwhelming, and I could do nothing but accept this. I needed to surrender to this and float.

If you face a rip tide or tsunami of challenges, the same steps apply to knowing you are not alone. Find your people and name where you are. If circumstances are so overwhelming and you have no ability to influence, then please know you have the power and ability to CHOOSE. Name what you need and you can float. Make sure the people who love and surround you know how they can support you. This can also look like finding a compassionate mental health professional. Please know this can be discouraging. It can be intense. This storm will eventually pass. There will be a time when you re-engage; it is ok to wait for the dynamics to calm down, and it is ok to care for yourself and your family. You will need your strength and a full gas tank for when the storm calms. This is a beautiful time to check out the toolkits. Whether it is the emotions of stress, guilt, or the need to create boundaries, use this time to rest and build the muscles you will need for the next phase of the journey.

As we weather the storms of caring for an aging parent, we confront our vulnerability and limitations with humility and grace. We acknowledge that we cannot do it alone and reach out for help and support when needed. In embracing our vulnerability, we discover the power of authenticity, the courage to show up as our true selves, flaws, and all, and to connect with others in genuine and meaningful ways.

In times of trial and adversity, we turn to our community for strength, support, and solace. Whether it is a support group for caregivers, a network of friends and family, or a community of faith, we find comfort in knowing that we are not alone. Together, we share our burdens, lift each other, and find hope and healing in the community bonds.

During the trials and tribulations, we find cause for celebration in the small victories that mark our progress along the journey. Whether it is a good day free from pain and suffering, a moment of clarity and connection with a loved one, or a milestone reached in their care and treatment, we pause to celebrate the moments of joy and triumph illuminating our path.

As we emerge from the storms of caring for our aging parents, we will emerge stronger, wiser, and more resilient than before. We carry with us the scars of battle and the seeds of hope—the belief that no matter how dark the night may seem, there is always light on the horizon.

In facing the storms of caring for our aging parent, we discover the depth of our courage, our compassion, and the human spirit's boundless capacity to endure, persevere, and thrive.

A MOMENT TO REFLECT

Okay. Are you ready? Let's invite some imagery into this reflection.

Imagine a future storm, something that represents your biggest fear or challenge with caring for your aging parent. Jot down your first thoughts.

Now take a moment to picture yourself navigating that storm applying each step of the PACE model: **Pause, Assess, Choose,** and **Embrace**.

How does moving through each step help you manage and thrive in the chaos?

CHAPTER 12

Finding Hope in the Dark Days

For many of us caring for our aging parents, faith in a higher power is a steadfast anchor in the stormy seas of uncertainty. Whether rooted in religious beliefs or spiritual convictions, faith provides solace, strength, and a sense of purpose in adversity.

Resilience is the ability to bounce back from hardship and the capacity to grow and thrive in the face of adversity. Providing support and care demands abundant resilience to navigate the journey's unpredictable twists and turns.

I have dear friends who head up a contemplative ministry and who often share practices that help me develop more reflective and spiritual practices. They shared with me a practice that was developed based on the stories of survivors of the Holocaust. I had a very dear friend, Leo Durlacher, who was a Holocaust survivor; because of him, I found this practice to be very meaningful and near to my heart. On the dark days when I am forced to move forward, this practice feels so grounded in a deep desire to survive that I can also find strength.

It has been said that on the walls of a concentration camp, these seventeen words were found.

Prepare	Listen	Smile
Care	Focus	Choose
Believe	Relax	Act
Forgive	Pray	Trust
Change	Risk	Accept
Persist	Wait	

These words were placed there as markers of hope and to help us lead centered lives rather than ones of despair.

The practice is to have the words somewhere on your wall. I placed mine in my laundry room as I am in this space every morning. You are encouraged to slowly read or even say these words out loud, as one of them might lift my spirits when a problem or a situation arises. I have found peace standing in front of these words, scanning them, and being open to which ones draw my attention. When I am able to sit with a word on my dark days, I can draw on the ability of this strategy to help me focus my energy and think forward rather than dwelling and getting stuck in the tough times I face un my day. This reframe is powerful and one I still use.

I share these seventeen words and this practice with you to encourage you to read them in moments of darkness and despair. They can help you find the light, even if only a glimmer, dear reader, and then turn to the light.

This journey is often fraught with spiritual challenges—questions of meaning, purpose, and the nature of suffering abound.

Community and fellowship play vital roles in sustaining us through our journey, providing support, encouragement, and a sense of belonging in times of need. Together, we can celebrate the importance of community sharing stories of camaraderie, solidarity, and mutual support through our connections with others, whether within religious communities, support groups, or social networks—we discover the power of collective resilience and the healing presence of compassionate companionship.

Hope is at the heart of faith and resilience, a radiant beacon that shines brightly in even the darkest times. Through stories of hope's triumph over despair and adversity, we celebrate the unwavering human spirit and the capacity for renewal and regeneration within each of us.

A MOMENT TO REFLECT

Take a pause here, just for a moment. **Sit with those seventeen words I mentioned earlier.** Consider them carefully. Focus on your breath and see what catches your attention.

Prepare	Listen	Smile
Care	Focus	Choose
Believe	Relax	Act
Forgive	Pray	Trust
Change	Risk	Accept
Persist	Wait	

Are there one or two words that bring you comfort or hope today? Jot the word (s) down on a piece of paper or make a note on your phone. Bring your attention to this word a few times throughout your day.

Consider how you might bring these markers of hope into your daily life, offering yourself space and grace along the way.

Imagine the impact of carrying one of these markers forward—whether it's resilience, compassion, or another word that resonates most deeply.

CHAPTER 13

The Demanding Rhythm

In the demanding rhythm of caring for our aging parents, the boundaries between personal and professional realms blur as crises and our responsibilities and obligations combine.

We have created reels on social media sharing some of these complex and painful moments of caring for aging parents, and the response and engagement of people have been powerful. In many comments, people asked, "How do you do it? "Who is supporting you? Who are you talking with? What are you reading? How are you able to find joy in the dark times?" I love it when people ask these big questions.

For many of us, this journey is not confined to the four walls of our homes but extends into the corridors of our workplaces. Balancing the needs of our loved ones with the demands of our careers can feel like walking a tightrope, each step fraught with uncertainty and tension. Yet, within this tension, we find the opportunity to cultivate resilience, resourcefulness, and compassion in the face of adversity.

We are accustomed to making sacrifices while caring for our aging parents. We find ourselves making tough decisions, whether they involve sacrificing our time, energy, or well-being. As we navigate these competing expectations, we must also face the realities of our professional responsibilities. From meetings to deadlines, presentations to promotions, the professional world moves forward, frequently oblivious to the challenges we endure in our personal lives. For me, the ability to work as a consultant was a vital component. I required flexibility. I needed the ability to work remotely. I'm sharing this to raise awareness among employers.

Many of us aged 45-to-65 require flexibility to care for our families. I hope the world becomes kinder and more sensitive to those of us who care for our family, including aging parents.

With competing priorities, striking a balance can feel like an impossible task. However, it is precisely in the chaos of our lives that we learn the strength of resilience and flexibility. Many times, this growth and transition could have been more seamless. In the heat of these situations, I had to learn how to set firmer limits, delegate duties, and seek help from coworkers and loved ones. I wouldn't say I like asking for assistance. I don't like admitting that I can't do everything alone. My growing pains have been consistent.

As a result, getting psychological support was critical to my capacity to weather the storms. My counselors have been lifelines to me. Learning to negotiate space between our personal and professional duties is an ongoing process. Powering up and having experience in those complex, sticky situations is crucial.

It is easy to overlook our well-being when dealing with the pressures of caring and professional life. Self-care is not a luxury but a necessary skill for negotiating the complexity of caring for our aging parents with grace and perseverance. From carving out time for solitude to indulging in soul-nourishing activities, self-care enables us to refill our reserves and tackle the difficulties of caring and professional life with newfound energy.

A humbling awakening for me was how quickly and rudely I was pulled away from my daily routine: from my need to travel to be with my aging parent to the mornings when I needed to jump onto calls and would be on the phone for hours to the unexpected disruptions of whatever flavor crisis each day brought. I was unaware that the daily habits that keep me healthy and strong as a mom and parent were suddenly gone. Here are some of the daily habits that fell away during the storms of my aging parent:

Morning Prayers	Morning Stretches
Eating Healthy Breakfast	Cup of Tea
Daily Bible Study	Walking the Dog
Eating Meals on Time	Movement
Call Family	Visits Friends
Doing Nothing!!!	Laughing
Dates with Hubby	Time Outside
Being in Nature	Sunshine

I was stunned when my life began to settle after years of these pieces missing. Being caught up in my journey, I stepped away from the activities that brought me joy and fueled my life. Our small daily habits are so important not only for our physical health but also for our mental health.

I am grateful to my counselor, who encouraged me to return to activities that bring me joy and happiness. What are you stepping away from? How might you build them back into your day? One of my first steps was re-establishing my morning routine, which included listening and singing to praise music as I started my day. This made an enormous difference. I encourage you to take one small step back to normal; you are worth it.

A MOMENT TO REFLECT

Okay, let's take a break and practice box breathing. Breath in, 1-2-3-4. Hold, 1-2-3-4. Breathe out, 1-2-3-4. Hold, 1-2-3-4. Repeat if you'd like. If not, let's move on.

What are some of the daily habits you are stepping away from? Jot down what comes to mind:

Here are some ideas:

Morning Prayers	Morning Stretches
Healthy Breakfast	Cup of Tea
Daily Bible Study	Walking the Dog
Eating Meals on Time	Movement
Call Family	Visits Friends
Doing Nothing!!!	Laughing
Dates with Hubby	Time Outside
Being in Nature	Sunshine

Now, consider what you have discovered: **what habits are missing, and how might you build** them back into your day?

What is ONE daily habit that you can do TODAY?

Who is a loved one or a friend who can help remind you to build back your daily habits?

CHAPTER 14

Finding Paths to Healing

One of the most significant challenges of this journey is learning to forgive ourselves for our perceived failings and shortcomings. Whether it is a missed appointment, a harsh word spoken in frustration, or a moment of weakness in the face of overwhelming stress, we must learn to extend the same compassion and forgiveness to ourselves that we offer to others. We release guilt and shame through self-forgiveness, freeing ourselves to heal and grow.

Caring for our loved ones will frequently strain our relationships with them as we manage the complexity of care and assistance in the face of disease and aging.

As tough as it is to recollect the waves of the storm and crisis, reflecting on and learning from this experience is crucial. Recalling conversations with my aged parent, siblings, and family in which I didn't present my best self is challenging. Trying to make judgments under severe pressure, functioning at an elevated level for my family and clients, and continuously being dragged down by the undertow of caring for my aging mom was beyond my ability. Being able to forgive myself and repair connections with my aging parents, spouse, immediate relatives, and siblings has been a primary focus. I'm still working on fixing those relationships.

I also need to forgive myself for the coping mechanisms I used to help get through these challenging times. Sometimes, I spend countless hours watching my favorite online shows, numerous hours on my phone, and other times drinking an extra glass of wine. Some days, I collapsed on the couch. I am trying to be kind to myself and say I did what I needed to do to cope with exceedingly tricky circumstances. I can now see that many of my coping behaviors don't serve me well, and I honestly don't need them anymore. Letting those behaviors go and learning to embrace life more healthfully is where I want to live my life.

As family caregivers, we may experience hints of resentment and animosity toward individuals we care for and even toward ourselves and others who may have contributed to our burden. We believe this is inevitable given the high demands placed on us. The first step is confronting challenging feelings, examining the sources of our wrath and bitterness, and discovering methods to release them with compassion and forgiveness. The practice of self-compassion—a profound love and acceptance of ourselves just as we are—is crucial to forgiveness and healing. We can recover when we cultivate self-compassion and treat ourselves with the same kindness, understanding, and support we do for others. Self-compassion gives us the fortitude to withstand the storms of caring for our elderly parents.

For many of us in the squeeze, we do our best to care for and support our families, careers, lives, and aging parents. This has meant many difficult choices of how I spend my time. Do I get to attend the prom photo event with my son, or do I attend to the crisis of my aging parent?

I have tried to forgive myself for all the missed moments and for not showing up as my best self. I have to be honest, this is still hard for me. Looking back over the last eight years, I find it easier to see where I fell short, where I missed out, and where I would have done things differently than all the small wins along the way. My husband and children have loved and supported me on my best and worst days.

The ability to be kinder to myself and LET GO of all the places I fell short is part of the ongoing healing. And not only is this healing for myself but also for all the relationships – like with your husband, children, siblings, friends, and extended family. When you go through this stage of caring for your aging parents and all the dynamics and challenges you will face, you come out of it differently on the other side. This changes you in ways you cannot even imagine. How do you reenter the world and the places you are shifting to? You are a different human than you were when the storms first struck.

I think this will be a perfect topic for a future book on how the heck one heals after caring for your aging parent's chapter closes. Stay tuned for that one!

Being able to move into a healing space, I looked to my wonderful counselor, who helped me develop goals with practical steps. Taking advantage of retreats, workshops, and fun days with my friends was all part of my healing recipe. I have to say the morning pass to the day spa and massages were beyond magical. Getting back in touch with ME about what I have been through and what I hope to do and be through was also part of the healing process.

Looking at how I have been coping and what serves me well and what doesn't serve me well was another part of my healing. I share it with the hope that you might be able to cast a vision for yourself of a day when you can lay down anything that you're carrying or escape behaviors that you're employing to help you get through these challenging times. I promise you that day will come, and my hope for you is that you can be healthier and more whole at that place and time in your journey.

A MOMENT TO REFLECT

One last time, let's focus and breathe for one minute. Get our minds centered as we prepare ourselves for what's next. **Think about where healing** might be calling to you in this season.

Where do you need to give yourself some grace, letting go of the pressure to have it all figured out? Imagine the difference it could make if you offered yourself a little more compassion and space.

As you reflect, consider your biggest takeaway here: what is one thing you can carry forward to bring a bit more grace into your journey?

Strength for the Journey Ahead

As you reach this point, we hope you feel a new strength taking root—a set of muscles built through what you've read and the insights you've gained.

Remember, this is just the beginning. We have spaces for you to connect, find support, and continue learning and places to share your voice and experiences with others walking a similar path.

We're so grateful you're here, and we're excited to hear from you—and from the friends you invite—about what's working and how it may inspire others along the way.

While our time together here is drawing to a close, our journey of caring for our parents continues. Each day presents us with new opportunities to gain knowledge, grow, and make a difference in the lives of those we care for. As we reflect on the insights gained and the connections forged, let us embrace hope and determination for the road ahead.

We hope this journey provides comfort, guidance, and support for you on your caregiving path. May its lessons stay with you as you navigate the challenges and joys that lie ahead with compassion and grace.

We hope you have found affirmation and language to describe the path you are walking. We hope that you see you are not alone. We hope you have found a framework that helps you as you care for your aging parents.

As we embark on this caregiving journey, may we embrace the complexity of caregiving with open hearts and open minds. May we honor the sacrifices of those who have come before us and pave the way for those who will follow us.

Let us find solace in the knowledge that, in caregiving, we discover not only the depths of our humanity but also the boundless capacity of the human spirit to endure, overcome, and thrive.

For me personally, I went to talk with my incredible counselor, Dr Barbara Martin, to share a story about when I visited my mom and brought a dear friend to meet her for the first time. Anxiety and worry began to bubble up in my body as I worried about how my parent would react in front of my dear friend. Dr. Martin pointed out that when I see my aging parent, I don't need to spin out of control with anxiety and get stuck in my head. I don't need to run through scenarios and plan for every one of those scenarios. I don't have to think of all the things that could go wrong and how I would solve them. For example, what happens if the visit goes badly? What if my aging parent is mean to my friend? What if my aging parent makes a scene?

My counselor permitted me to HIT THE PAUSE BUTTON—
I can pause on all the anxiety, thinking, and energy I used to
invest in these interactions. Instead, I might see myself as a
repair person. When I go to the door of my aging parent, I can
come fully present and ready for whatever I encounter. I bring
my toolbox with tools I have learned from my lived experience,
collaborating with my counselor, and the countless books I have
read on this topic. I have what I need in my toolbox to
appropriately respond to situations and the stress of caregiving.
This was yet another gift that I needed to add to my toolbox.
My prayer is that the caregiving journey gives you what you
need for your toolbox to find peace and joy while caring for
your aging parents.

But our journey doesn't end here; it is just the beginning. As we
conclude this guide, we invite you to heed a call to action to
continue spreading kindness, empathy, and support to those in
need. Whether listening to one caring for their aging parent,
advocating for better resources in our communities, or simply
offering a helping hand to someone struggling, every act of
kindness matters.

As we each go out into the world...

*Let us create spaces where those caring for aging parents
are seen, valued, and supported.*

*Let us be a beacon of light for others facing similar
challenges.*

Let us make a meaningful impact on those we care for and the world around us.

We are sending you our light & love on your journey...

May your path be filled with moments of kindness, compassion, and connection.

May you always remember that it's okay to name and honor your struggles.

May you always remember that it's okay to ask for help and accept help from others.

May you find ways to permit yourself to take care of yourself.

May you know that you do not walk this path of caring for your aging parents alone.

Our hope is that we can thrive in chaos, working together to name this stage of life and make it markedly better for the next generation! - Heather & Jayne

Our Work Continues

We have heard from readers that after finishing the book, they want to go deeper and first action steps. Our work continues as we are in the process of publishing our next book, *Living in the Sticky, Tricky, and Sometimes Icky Toolkit*. This book is a toolkit full of tips and suggestions on how to handle all those situations and conversations that are so darn hard. We name the tensions for the aging parents, we name the tensions for the adult children or family caregivers, and we offer actionable first steps to move forward! Our readers have shared that this is like having a friend who is standing by at the ready for whatever tricky situation pops up with your aging parent.

We have also heard from readers who desire to further explore the resources we shared in the book. Feel free to use the QR code below to visit our website, PeopleInTheSqueeze.com. As more and more people are asking for resources, the research and resources that are becoming available are dynamic. You can follow People in the Squeeze on IG or TT as we frequently create content that will point you to what is emerging and developing in the space that helps us all better navigate the care of our aging parents. To that point – we'd love to hear from you!

While we have shared some in-the-squeeze moments we've found to be sticky, tricky, and icky, we know you have your own stories, your moments of "Is that a red flag, or just a weird Tuesday?"

If you've seen any signs, clues, or curious behaviors from your loved ones—maybe a refrigerator packed with ancient condiments or keys found in the dishwasher—we want to hear about them. Perhaps you've uncovered small, poignant moments that hint at bigger needs. Please share it with us.

Head over to our website, PeopleInTheSqueeze.com, where we have created a place for you to share your stories, insights, and laughter-filled experiences. Subscribe to our Substack, People in the Squeeze, where others share their candid and personal stories, revealing the humor and humanity in the challenges of caring for aging parents.

Let's build a space brimming with shared wisdom, real-life examples, and even a laugh or two because navigating this journey together makes it all a little bit easier for us.

REFERENCES

Books:

Hochschild, A. R., & Machung, A. (1989). *The second shift: Working families and the revolution at home*. Viking.

Schor, J. B. (1992). *The overworked American: The unexpected decline of leisure*. Basic Books.

Sheehy, G. (1976). *Passages: Predictable crises of adult life*. E. P. Dutton.

Mace, N. L., & Rabins, P. V. (1981). *The 36-hour day: A family guide to caring for people who have Alzheimer's disease, related dementias, and memory loss*. Johns Hopkins University Press.

Reports and Articles:

AARP & National Alliance for Caregiving. (2020, May). *Caregiving in the United States 2020*. AARP. https://doi.org/10.26419/ppi.00103.003

Britton, L. E., Kaur, G., Zork, N., Marshall, C. J., & George, M. (2023). "We tend to prioritize others and forget ourselves": How women's caregiving responsibilities can facilitate or impede diabetes self-management. *Diabetic Medicine*. Advance online publication. https://doi.org/10.1111/dme.14992

El Issa, E. (2024, April). *2024 financially assisting aging parents report.* NerdWallet. Retrieved from
https://www.nerdwallet.com

Mallapaty, S. (2024, August 29). Humanity's newest brain gains are most at risk from ageing. *Nature.*
https://doi.org/10.1038/d41586-024-02784-w

Maslach, C., & Leiter, M. P. (2016). Understanding the burnout experience: Recent research and its implications for psychiatry. *World Psychiatry, 15*(2), 103–111. https://doi.org/10.1002/wps.20311

National Council on Aging. (2022, October). *Caregiver stress: The impact on physical health.* Retrieved from
https://www.ncoa.org/article/caregiver-stress-the-impact-on-physical-health/

Peters, R. (2006). Aging and the brain. *Postgraduate Medical Journal,* 82(964), 84–88. https://doi.org/10.1136/pgmj.2005.036665

Schaeffer, K., & Aragao, C. (2023, May 9). *Key facts about moms in the United States.* Pew Research Center. Retrieved from
https://www.pewresearch.org

Silverstein, M., & Giarrusso, R. (2010). Multigenerational stress: A decade-long study of aging and family life. *Journal of Marriage and Family,* 72(3), 595–611. https://doi.org/10.1111/j.1741-3737.2010.00722.x

Stress Measurement Network. (n.d.). *Caregivers stress.* National Institute on Aging, University of California, San Francisco. Retrieved from https://www.stressmeasurement.org

Schiano, B. (2021, May). *Give your brain a break—Course design tips to avoid feeling overwhelmed: 5 questions to ask yourself when planning for a new semester.* Harvard Business Publishing Education. Retrieved from https://hbsp.harvard.edu/inspiring-minds/course-design-tips-to-avoid-feeling-overwhelmed

White, G. B. (2015, December 14). The invisible work that women do around the world. *The Atlantic.* Retrieved from https://www.theatlantic.com/business/archive/2015/12/the-invisible-work-that-women-do-around-the-world/420372/

World Health Organization. (2022, October 17). *Menopause.* Retrieved from https://www.who.int

www.ingramcontent.com/pod-product-compliance
Lightning Source LLC
Chambersburg PA
CBHW051627120626
46551CB00014B/1971